The ABC's of Homeschooling

by

Laura Ann Huber

TELEMACHUS
PRESS

THE ABC'S OF HOMESCHOOLING

Cover designed by Carolyn Doll

Cover Art by Carolyn Doll

Author's website
http://www.laurahuber.com

Published by Telemachus Press, LLC
http://www.telemachuspress.com

ISBN #978-1-937387-90-7 (eBook)
ISBN #978-1-937387-91-4 (paperback)

Version 2011.11.29

Printed in the United States of America

10 9 8 7 6 5 4 3 2 1

To my three children:
Keith, Kristin, and Elijah,
Even though I am considered by many to be your teacher, you have taught me more about life, love, and happiness than you'll ever imagine. This book would never have existed without you. You are all wonderful children, and I am mesmerized by the amazing people you are becoming.

To my husband:
Bryon,
You have provided well for our family, always giving of yourself, and enabling me to stay home with our children. Even though at times we could have used extra income you never once asked me to help. Because of your dedication to me and our children this book was able to manifest. I truly could not have done any of this without your love and support. Thank you for putting me through writing school and believing in me. You are the love of my life, my rock – my soul mate. Thank you for taking a chance on me and allowing me to be who I am.

Best Wishes,

Laura Huber

With Thanks and Appreciation

First, I must thank my Creator, for waking me up at 3:30 in the morning and providing not only the idea and title for this book, but all of the principles as well. I am also grateful to you, God, for putting the perfect people in my life at the perfect time. Thank you for giving me signs, whenever I asked if I was on the right path. Steve Himes – you were my first sign.

Next, I must thank my sister for listening to me rattle on about this book, the next book(s), my life, and my dreams. Mary Lou, you are the best sister and friend anyone could ever hope for. No matter how bad a day I'm having you can always make me laugh and feel better. Your excitement and belief in what I'm doing is a great inspiration and keeps me on track. Thank you also for encouraging me to go after my dreams and keep believing.

Thanks to my parents Alma and Frank Simmermeyer, you are always a constant source of strength and encouragement whenever I need a little extra boost. You have taught me how to be a virtuous woman by constantly showing me shining examples of how to live my life. Mom, if it wasn't for your continuing prompting, even after I had a family, I would never have picked up my pen to write this book. Dad, you taught me how to go after my dreams and believe in myself, even though the odds were stacked against me. I am truly grateful to have such wonderful parents.

Thanks to Nancy Grunkemeyer, my nana, at age 89, you are still an inspiration. I love the fact that I can tell everyone that my nana edited this book. It was no small task. Your well-advised suggestions were all made. Nana, you are amazing. Grammar, punctuation and vocabulary errors do not stand a chance against you and your pen. I am even going thank you for correcting my grammar when I was a child – even though I didn't appreciate it then – I do now. I still think of your home on the farm, and will do many things for my grandkids like you did for us.

Aunt Jane, thank you for all of the research, help, and inspiration you have given me over the years. Your enthusiasm and cheerful way of giving of yourself makes any job go much smoother. All of your love and support is greatly appreciated.

My neighbor Martha, you were the first one to read this book. I was really inspired by your raving reviews. Thanks, not only for encouraging me, but for all those borrowed "cups of sugar" and always being there at a moment's notice.

Many thanks to all of my very close friends who have all supported me and believed in me. The encouragement I receive from each of you made me believe in myself enough to write this book and others. Every one of you teaches me something different and important about myself, and I treasure all of you. It is said that you can learn a lot about a person by the friends she keeps. That statement makes me feel extremely good about myself. Thanks to all of you for allowing me to be your friend. You know who you are:)

Thanks to Carolyn Doll, my graphic artist. I appreciate all those extra hours you put in to make the cover of this book eye-catching and perfect. You are not only a great artist but a good friend as well.

Kim Thompson, my photographer, thank you for coming to my home at a moment's notice. You have been down this road with me before. Your keen eye and expertise makes everyone and everything look great. I'm glad we're friends.

Thank you Mike Mulligan, my business adviser, you kept me on the right track, at the right pace, when I wanted to veer off and go too fast. Because of your advice, vigilance, and research I ended up succeeding.

Vinny, at IMI Software, I appreciate your one on one advice, and being so understanding and patient with all my questions. You encouraged me that together we could build a website in less than two weeks and we did! Your advice really helped out when I needed it most.

Thanks to everyone at Telemachus Press, my "partner's" in publishing: Steve Jackson, Steve Himes and all the rest working behind the scenes to make my book a success. I appreciate the way you immediately made me feel important. I am truly grateful to you for raising the bar in the ever growing and changing world of publishing.

Because of all of the wonderful people in my life, and my deep faith in God, I am able to live the life of my dreams. Thanks to all who have brought me to where I am today.

The ABC's of Homeschooling

Attitude is the crowning glory of your home.
Choose well and it will protect you from many of life's storms.
Behavior, whether good or bad, will open and close many doors
to life's opportunities and possibilities.
Combining, condensing, and containing will make
entering your home a much more enjoyable and comforting experience.

TABLE OF CONTENTS

Introduction

Now, more than ever before, parents are intrigued and enticed with the prospect of homeschooling their children. Today, over two million families in the United States are choosing to homeschool, and that number is expected to increases by five to eight percent every year. In September of 1999, I started homeschooling our oldest child, Keith. The idea of homeschooling was not nearly as common or accepted back then. Homeschooling was never something I thought I could do, but it did interest me. Fortunately, I had friends and mentors who were well seasoned and experienced, when it came to homeschooling, so I solicited their advice. Having the counsel of these women was invaluable to me in the beginning days. It gave me the confidence and courage I needed to get started. When times were tough and I questioned my ability to teach my children at home, they assured me that I was doing the right thing. That was over twelve years ago. It's hard for me to believe I've been homeschooling our three children for that length of time, and now parents seek my advice.

More and more often I am approached by parents who come to me and say, "You have such wonderful, well-rounded children, how do you do it?" (This is a statement that never gets old.) My answer to them is, "It's easier than you think if you have a good foundation in place." In order to have a strong house that will withstand many storms, the Bible teaches us to build our homes on rock and not shifting sand. By applying the principles in this book all parents – not just the ones who choose to homeschool, will put down a strong foundation for their family life. Once this is in place anything is possible.

There is no right or wrong way to read this book. You do not have to read it from front to back. You can look over the table of contents and start reading whatever seems to be most interesting to you at the time. I'm all about being flexible whenever possible – however, every principle set forth is important and should be followed to the best of your ability, if you want to raise happy, independent children in a fun and orderly atmosphere. Yes, there will be some rough days. Everyone – even parents who send their children to school have bad days. Learn how our family gets through them. There is even a section on how my youngest son overcame his dyslexia.

Homeschooling is, and should be, as diverse as the people around the world, and although there is no exact science for homeschooling, the doctrine in this book is very important and basic information to fit into each family's unique lifestyle. Every family is drawn to different techniques and resources. You will find what works best for your family only by trial and error. What works for one child or family may or may not work for you. I do not suggest a specific curriculum, but give examples as to what I do, and direct you to places and resources to help you make up your own mind.

If you, like over two million families in the United States, decide to homeschool, I promise you will not be disappointed in this book. Start reading and lay down a good foundation for your children. Then watch as they blossom into wonderful independent people. Believe me when I say, "It's easier than you think."

"Let's start at the very beginning. It's a very good place to start.
When you read you begin with ABC ..."
When you homeschool you begin with ATTITUDE.

A = ATTITUDE and AUTHORITY

ATTITUDE

"I learned good spirits and optimism can carry the day."

Martha Stuart

Before you ever get out of bed in the morning your attitude will start off the day right or wrong. It's true, "if momma ain't happy, ain't nobody happy." A sure fire way to wake up in a good mood every day is to have a rejuvenating morning routine.

Each person will have his/her own personal preference, but there are a few acts everyone should complete before starting the day.

1. Thank your Creator. (Ex. "Thank you, God, for this day, my family, home, etc.") You must establish an "attitude of gratitude" before arising. This sets the standards for the day. If you think an "attitude of fortitude" is better—think again. Focus on being grateful and I assure you your day will be incredible. Try it!

2. Stretch. My daughter's 85-year-old ballet teacher taught me this. She was more nimble than the 30-year-old mothers of her students. To open up your lungs and get your blood pumping, reach for the sky. Touch your toes, coming up very slowly one vertebra at a time. Rotate your shoulders a few times. Bring both arms around your back as far as you can. (*This is the minimum amount of stretching you should do.*) Don't worry if you hear snap, crackle, or pop—this is normal—at least that's what I hear some mornings.

3. Have a plan for your day. This should actually be completed the night before, if it isn't, now is the time to make one. If it is, now is the time to look it over and revise if necessary.

I have created a planner to help keep you focused on what you really want to accomplish everyday called, *The Life Planner—Discovering Yourself and Achieving Your Goals.* You can receive free downloadable pages at www.laurahuber.com or purchase a copy to make it easier on yourself. This is a calendar type day planner to keep you focused on goals that will make a difference in your life. Pat Riley tells us, "Shoulda, coulda, and woulda won't get it done. In attacking adversity, only a positive attitude, alertness, and regrouping to basics can launch a comeback."

Many people fail to realize that outside circumstances aren't nearly as important as how we feel on the inside. God gave us dominion over the earth and our feelings. Pay attention to your feelings they are meant to guide you and be your life barometer. No one, repeat, NO ONE can make you feel a certain way unless you allow it. I once heard a story about a man in a Nazi prison camp. We all know for a fact that those conditions were the worst in the history of the world. But this certain person refused to allow the guards and terrible treatment of his human companions to control his feelings. He knew his feelings were the only things he could control. No one will ever know why, but for some reason unknown to the logical world, the guards treated him better than the other prisoners. Now, I'm not saying his stay was pleasant, by all means, but I am saying that he controlled his attitude, changing his circumstances for the better in the grimmest situation. Martha Washington said, "I learned from experience that the greater part of our happiness or misery depends on our dispositions and not our circumstances"

Your attitude decides the course of your life and ultimately makes an impact on your children. Look around you. What makes you happy? Think about those things. What needs to be changed? Maybe just your attitude. Dr. Wayne Dyer says, "When you change the way you look at things, the things you look at change." Start now with a happy disposition. If you're really not happy, smile anyway. Fake it until you make it. Just thinking about smiling makes my attitude improve. If you notice that you need a pick-me-up, ask yourself a few questions, "Am I hungry? Do I just need a hot cup of tea or coffee? Am I overwhelmed?" Maybe you just need to pamper yourself a little. Allowing the children to sleep in for thirty more minutes might be all it takes to make the day run smoother.

Many days I wake up in a good mood, but one of my children doesn't. Most of the time your attitude can change theirs. Smile, be patient, change the subject to something they like or are more interested in. Sometimes the child just needs a little more attention. However, DO NOT let the child continue in a bad mood for long and always remember—YOU ARE IN CHARGE AND IN CONTROL—even when you don't feel like it. If cajoling and kindness isn't working, it's time to separate the child from the rest of the family and maybe even use a "time out" session. If a child seems extremely agitated he may just need a bit of exercise. If you live in the country send him outside to run around for a bit to get some of that pent up energy out. He will feel much better when he comes back in. If all of the above fail to appease the bad attitude

it's time to bring out the BIG GUNS ... put the child back to bed
for fifteen minutes to one hour. This tactic has always worked for
me. It refreshes the child and gives mom a break from the
monotony of the morning. If you have other children, you can now
concentrate on them. If you have only one, you're free to do
something you want until the child wakes up.

All of us get tired and grumpy from time to time and just need
to be pampered or get some extra sleep. Of course, this is not
normal behavior. Most of the time children and parents should
both wake up in a good mood. If you don't there could be
something wrong at a deeper level and life needs to be re-
evaluated. Try to get to the bottom of, *why*, if a bad attitude will not
go away. The answer could be as simple as better nutrition. (We'll
discuss this more in the chapter on Nutrition.)

*"I am convinced that life is 10% what happens to me and 90% how I react to
it. And so it is with you ... we are in charge of our attitude."*

Charles R. Swindoll

AUTHORITY
"Unthinking respect for authority is the greatest enemy of truth."

Albert Einstein

It is true, the above quote. To take for granted what someone of
authority tells you can indeed be catastrophic to your well-being.
Doctors can be wrong. Teachers can be wrong. Parents can be
wrong. Even presidents of great countries can be wrong. But the
fact is we need authority. Someone has to take responsibility and
take charge, but many people would much rather allow someone
else to make decisions for them. Is it because we don't want to be
responsible if something goes wrong? Maybe it's because you were
scared of people in positions of authority when you were a child,
and think if you show authority, children will run in fear when they

see you coming? It's really quite the opposite. Children live to please people of authority.

Sometimes we see people of authority like our parents, preachers, teachers, doctors, coaches … and their role of authority, as being the only part of them. They may seem hardened or uncaring at times. We forget they are human and have feelings and lives just like us. It's always funny when my husband and I go out for the evening in our small town. He has coached pee-wee football for many years. The young boys are amazed to see him somewhere besides on the football field. They look at him sheepishly, like children visiting with Santa Claus. One boy was extremely shocked when he saw me with him, and asked in an astonished voice. "You have a wife?" I'm sure this child did not realize his coach had not only a *wife* but a *life* away from the football field.

Look around you. Do you think the majority of children respect their parents and think of them as a person of authority? Have you ever witnessed a situation where the child made a total fool of a well-meaning, loving parent? I have—many times. Why are we as a nation not only intimidated of people in authority, but also afraid to take the role of authority in any part of life, including parenting? Do you, like so many others think it's the "in thing" to allow your children to think you're a fool? It is appalling to me how most sitcoms nowadays show the father figure as a bumbling idiot. It can be funny to watch, but if mother or father want respect from their children this is not the way to achieve it.

For parents, authority is like walking a tight rope one hundred feet above sea level without a net, while hungry lions are waiting for our dissension to the hard packed earth. We have to maintain a good balance between allowing our children to make decisions on their own and presenting ourselves as an approachable and kind authority figure. Quite a feat indeed!

So, how do we as parents accomplish this tight rope act without falling to the lions? First of all you must like and respect yourself. If you do not like and respect yourself, everyone, including your children, will pick up on it. Notice I said LIKE. Not love. Children will love you no matter what kind of parent you are—it is their nature. But if you don't like and respect yourself chances are no one else will either. Next, you MUST have self-confidence. If you are wishy-washy on decisions and waver back and forth, everyone—especially your children will sense it and pounce on you, wearing down your authority and diminishing your respect. One of the things my mother would say to me when I kept asking, "Why?" and she didn't have an answer was, "Because, I'm the mom!" I absolutely hated when she said this. I thought to myself, what kind of an answer is that? It makes no sense. But now it makes all the sense in the world. She was establishing herself as a person of authority. Sometimes we can explain and explain to our children why—and they still will not see it our way.

When you establish yourself as an authority it doesn't mean that children won't try to challenge you. I can guarantee if you have children, you will be challenged. Here is an example of an argument I recently had with one of my teenagers. "Why are you taking a break already? We just got started." I say. "I already finished my job," is the reply. "No, I told you to look on the list when you finished your first job." "No, you didn't." "Yes, I did." Back and forth it goes. Finally, I say, "This is a disrespectful way to speak to your mother. If you have an important thing to argue about, I want to hear what you have to say, your opinion is very important to me. Otherwise you need to respect me and do as you are told."

Establishing yourself as a person of authority means making decisions and sticking to them. Setting boundaries and rules and making sure they are obeyed. But it also means, listening to your children and asking their opinions. Being willing to compromise or even change your position if it is for the greater good of the child or family, and yes, even admitting that you are wrong from time to time. Show your children how to relate to you and others in authority with a comfortable respect by setting an example and encouraging them to do the same. In doing so, you will ensure for your children a future of success.

Pray for guidance before making all decisions—especially big ones, and ask your Higher Power to guide you and your family. Then believe without a shadow of a doubt you are being guided. This is very hard for a loving parent. You want only what is best for the child. You are afraid of making the wrong decision. I know, because just writing this makes me think of some of the hard decision making I've had to do. It can be very scary, but someone *must* be in control.

In the Bible, Jesus compares people to sheep. Did you know that the whole sheep herd will follow a leader even if it means falling off a cliff to its death? A sheep doesn't think for himself. You must think for yourself. Stand up for what you believe is right. If you fall off the tight rope of authority from time to time, just remember to catch yourself before you fall to the lions; then climb back up.

"There are two types of people who never amount to much; those who cannot do what they are told and those who can do nothing else."

Cyrus H. Curtis

B = BEHAVIOR

"Behavior is a mirror in which everyone displays his own image."

Johann Wolfgang von Goethe

It is very important to not only teach children academics, but etiquette and manners as well. Homeschooled children can and must be an example to other children in a society of sarcasm and crumbling conduct. If you happen to be out and about with your children during public school hours you must know that the general public, which I call the *Better Behavior Bureau*, will be watching your children out of the corner of their eyes, taking mental notes and thinking to themselves, "I wonder if these kids are homeschooled?" If your children are causing a disturbance, all homeschooled children's reputation will be on the line. Homeschooling today is much more acceptable than it was when I began twelve years ago, but many people still don't agree with this choice of education. Teach your children to be a shining example for all children not just homeschooled ones.

The best way to teach children good behavior is to set boundaries early. Dr. James Dobson a well-known author, psychologist, and founder of *Focus on the Family* taught me that if we discipline children early and often by the time they are five we won't have too much to correct anymore. I followed his advice and gave my children "loving discipline" when they were small. By the time they were in kindergarten little discipline was needed. It is much easier to teach a toddler right from wrong than it is a teen. If you make the child understand why the rule is in place, and show him respect and trust, then most of the time children are glad to obey rules. An example, we live in the country, in a very small town, but very close to the road. We are the only house around for about a half a mile. I taught my children at a young age that the road and front yard were off limits. I explained to them the dangers of going into the front yard without a trusted adult. We made an invisible boundary line in the back yard with landmarks to help. I explained that they could play outside and have lots of freedom but it was very dangerous for them to cross the invisible boundary line, and told them if they disobeyed the rule they would not have the freedom of coming and going outside whenever they wished. I checked their whereabouts carefully and often. Even though they did not know I was watching—they never crossed the invisible line. I don't want anyone to think it is going to be a piece of cake after the child turns five. Discipline is always challenging no matter what age your children are, but setting the standards early as to what is expected of them is much easier on everyone.

Children are so much smarter than we give them credit for. By explaining dangers and stating why they can or cannot do certain things they will understand and obey rules better and without as much resentment than if we lay down rules without explanation. Parenting is always a work in progress. I like to use TV and other children's bad behavior to teach mine about the importance of good behavior. If we are watching a TV program and the kids in the show aren't behaving appropriately, I point it out by saying something like, "That wasn't a very nice thing for her to say to her hard-working father." or, "That boy must not respect himself or others." If children see other kids behaving badly and haven't been instructed on what is right or wrong how will they know? When my two older children were five and six they attended a supervised activity that I chose not to attend. When they came home they talked a mile a minute about how they didn't like the bad behavior of the other children. I was concerned that I had created children that were too judgmental, so I asked one of the supervising adults what went on. She assured me that my children were correct in their judgment and were some of the few who did obey that night.

Interestingly, in the animal kingdom bad behavior can happen when adults are not monitoring the behavior of their young, also. Some time ago my family and I watched a documentary on elephants. Because of the depleting rain forest, families of elephants were moved by helicopter from their home to another place. About ten juvenile males were placed in their own territory away from the older adults. These young pachyderms caused a great deal of trouble, knocking down trees for fun, bullying rhinos—even killing one. As scientists watched they knew something must be done to stop the misbehaving teenage elephants. They decided to move some older males in with the younger ones. To the scientists delight and amazement the older elephants put a halt to the bad deeds of their offspring.

Deep down children really want to know you are in control and making sure their behavior is acceptable, giving them confidence and a sense of security. (You may never get them to admit this.) An example of this happened a couple of weeks ago while attending my fourteen-year-old son's baseball game. A girl in the crowd was shouting horrible and obnoxious words bordering on pornographic. It was absolutely awful and appalling. Everyone was so shocked; no one really knew what to do. Our umpires are just young teenage boys themselves, and hadn't been instructed on what to do in a case like this. It was so bad my mother-in-law actually called the police, but the man on duty did not come. I told her I was going over to confront and stop the girl. She begged me not to do it. She said the girl had a really bad reputation, and was afraid I would get hurt. Out of respect for her I, like everyone else, did nothing. After the game was over, and the boys were gathering their things, the girl continued to harass and cuss, hurling disgusting suggestions. This was ridiculous. I could take no more, besides my mother-in-law had already left and couldn't stop me this time. If the girl attacked me I really didn't care at this point. I told her in no uncertain terms, with the authority of Queen Elizabeth herself, to shut her mouth and leave. To my amazement she did just exactly as she was told, almost running away. Even more shocking to me was how the boys on the team reacted. Some boys even came up and thanked me, telling me she was like this at school and they wished the teachers would stand up to her the way I did. Is there an adult on the planet that thought she could become a hero among teens by confronting the bad behavior of one of them and putting an end to it? Kids want rules and action taken for bad behavior and this life experience of mine proves it.

One thing to always keep in mind when disciplining and setting the standards for your child's behavior is to always—no matter what—do it with love. My mother had a plaque hanging on a wall in our living room that read, "Do Everything with Love". Back when I was a child, it was more common for parents to spank their children. Guess what my loving mother used when her children misbehaved? The "Do Everything with Love" plaque. It stung a bit, but my siblings and I turned out alright. I could count on one hand how many times my mother actually used it on our backsides. Mostly she just had to point to it and we knew she meant business. One mysterious, dark night the "Do Everything with Love" plaque disappeared never to be found again. My sister and I suspect our brothers buried it in the backyard; after all, mom used it a little more on them than on us. There have been times during the duration of my motherhood that I myself have wanted to ask mom and dad if I could try finding it back again by digging up their yard. It's kind of a bittersweet icon of days gone by. And yes, even though I got spanked or my behavior put in check, I always knew my parents loved and respected me. We still enjoy a wonderful relationship and the love and respect for each other grows more every year.

Today, many more liberal thinkers say putting down rules stifles a child. I couldn't disagree more. When a child knows the rules to keep him and others safe and happy—and obeys them—he can enjoy much more freedom and so will his parents. You don't need a lot of rules; you just need a few clear and distinctive ones that the child understands, knowing action will be taken if they are not obeyed.

Reading some books on manners together will help both parents and children learn long forgotten rules on etiquette. After I started homeschooling my children I learned a lot about polite manners of society that I didn't even know existed. Chances are you yourself could brush up on this subject and improve your own behavior when you are teaching your children the proper way to behave. Did you know that when walking down a sidewalk or hall it is proper to always stay to your right? Do you know the proper way to introduce people to each other? Good behavior goes beyond not arguing in public and obeying rules. Sometimes it's knowing what to say and how to say it.

"Good manners will open doors that the best education cannot."

Clarence Thomas

C = COMBINE, CONDENSE, AND CONTAIN

"Cleanliness and order are not matters of instinct; they are matters of education, and like most great things, you must cultivate a taste for them."

Benjamin Disraeli

Who knew that "cleanliness and order" were matters of education? I sure never thought of it this way, but I also know that you will not run an efficient academic program without these in place. Today is the day you must start thinking about how to bring order to your home. If you are one of those people who maintain a well-balanced home in perfect order, you may skip this chapter. If on the other hand your home could use someone to come in and overhaul the clutter—I'm here to help.

Take a deep breath. You can do this. I'll be holding your hand every step of the way. Please don't get the wrong impression and think that my home is clutter-free. I can assure you it is not. Even though our house is large there is not much storage space. The basement is actually an old root cellar that stays damp, even with a dehumidifier running non-stop. Before my husband built bookshelves on either side of our fireplace, I really had to get inventive to keep everything organized. After remodeling for over nineteen years, I have become the queen of arrangement and containment. At one point I took all my antique dishes out of the china cabinet and used it for a bookcase. I even had a dresser in our living room that served as the place to store each individual child's school things. Each kid had a drawer of his/her own. Pens and pencils and extra school things were stored in a smaller top drawer. Everything was easy to get to and everyone always knew where everything was. Today, I am blessed with custom book shelves and built in desks, but our dining room still doubles as a school room, library, and office. However, I do know where everything is, at a moment's notice. (Most of the time!) :-)

Children thrive in orderly environments, and so do their mothers. There is nothing more aggravating when you're in the middle of a geometry lesson and can't find a protractor, even though you know very well you bought each child one at the beginning of the school year. Wasting precious time finding the protractor will get even the best student out of the mood for math.

This is where the 3 C's come into play. **CAUTION: If you've never cleaned out your closets or school things before, this could take some time.** If you can't block off at least a couple of hours of your schedule for this activity, you may want to designate a room or dining table to store piles while you work at will.

COMBINE

You must start with combine. Do this by combining like items together, and items that belong to a certain person. For example: If Kristin received glitter markers from Aunt Lou, these go into her pile. If there are markers that no one claims, but can be useful for everyone, these go in the marker pile. Start small. Some of the piles you may want to make are: Paper. Then designate, scrap paper, construction paper, lined paper, etc. Pens and Pencils. Ask yourself, "Are these for art or writing?" Put into appropriate piles. How about all those clippings and magazine articles or those cards you received in the mail for free with facts about dinosaurs or history? Designate a pile for each subject of interest to you or children and we'll talk about what to do with them later. Reference books. I have all my reference books combined by subject. If someone wants to know who St. Patrick was, I can go right to the books on saints and pick one out immediately. Teacher books. Maps. Are you getting the idea? Okay. Get started.

CONDENSE

Now that everything is combined into neat little piles of ownership or like things, it's time to condense. You may want to get the kids to help out at this point. Check each pen and marker and make sure it works. Pitch pens, pencils, markers and crayons that have given their all and have no life left. There is nothing more aggravating than seeing a nice, fat, black, sharpie marker—grabbing it to complete a poster—and it's all dried out. Darn, the rotten luck! Pitching now saves pain and confusion later. While condensing you must start asking questions like, "Is it useful?" "Do I have a duplicate that someone else could use?" If so bless them with it. "Do I really need four books on bugs?" Maybe, two would be enough. It's time to decide. Use the method called KISS. Which translates to: Keep It Simple Sally. Or Jane, whatever your name might be.

CONTAIN

Once you have condensed all of your piles, it's time to contain. That means finding the perfect home for all of those things you just deemed useful enough to stay. This part can be tricky. It is really a matter of choice when it comes to containing. I personally like to use antiques because I live in a house that was built in 1862. For me finding things at yard sales and flea markets is a better choice than plastic containers. No matter what kind of containers you choose to contain your piles, they must be convenient and efficient. This means things are easy to get to and very accessible or no one will ever put it back in the designated spot. If a basket, with a lid, looks nice sitting under the desk and can perfectly hold all the art supplies and is convenient—you have just found a perfect home for crafts. However, if your daughter is constantly getting into the art basket, and is having a difficult time, it is not the perfect home. Maybe an open basket on a bookshelf would be better for now.

As for all those loose papers clipped from magazines and different resources—purchase a three-ring binder. Buy some folders to fill it with. You may even be able to find folders with pictures on them to match the subject it is to contain. Example: If you've clipped neat nature articles, you might find a folder with a beautiful waterfall or mountain. You could even buy plain folders and glue a picture onto it that matches the subject inside. Buy a three ring hole punch. Instead of storing all the clippings inside folders, punch holes on the sides of the articles that are complete pages and store them inside a binder the way you would loose-leaf paper. Make sure to keep craft clippings separate from interesting facts about bugs, either by using the folders to divide or buying subject dividers. As for the free informative cards in the mail? Punch a hole in the top left corner and the bottom left corner of each card. Purchase key rings for each subject. Slide the cards onto the key ring. Now the cards can be stored and used like a book. Hint. Make sure to go in far enough so key ring doesn't cut through the edges of the cards.

Each child doesn't necessarily need his or her own desk but, it is important that children have a specific place to call their own to keep their own school things in order. Maybe like me, you could use an old dresser, giving each child an assigned drawer, or maybe each person could have a specific place on a nearby bookshelf. You decide what works best in your home. If you can afford it, now is the time to think about buying a neat pencil bag for each child or a plastic container they can decorate with markers, glitter, and stickers. Inside they can keep their own erasers, pencils, crayons, etc. This will go into the child's individual place along with his or her own school books. That way if your sons chew on pencils, and it makes your daughter sick to touch them, there won't be a problem. Some children are neat by nature and some are not. This keeps each one from feeling overwhelmed by the other. It also gives the child a feeling that he or she is more in control of their own life. If children share school books, allow one to store the science book, the other history according to their preference.

"What about all those art papers, crafts, and science projects?" Believe me I hear your pain. Take two large poster boards and tape one of the long edges and the two short edges together with duct tape. You've just created a place to put art pictures that can be stored under a bed or behind the family's sofa. As for all those other projects? I suggest taking pictures and making a file on the computer for each child and tossing the real stuff unless it is really something special. You must do this in a delicate way, being very careful of young children's feelings. If they've worked really hard on something don't toss it the next day. It's best to wait until the child has forgotten about it and moved on to create something new. I also have a square plastic container with a lid containing each child's mementos, birthday cards, First Communion certificates, and any school work they're proud of. We all know this should actually be in nice albums—and I truly wish it were—but the truth is I haven't gotten that organized—yet.

A great way to keep older children's school assignments in order is to buy a five subject notebook for each child. All their papers stay in one place and when you are going over studies with them, it's easy to flip to the next section when it's time for the next subject. We like, *Top Flight-Orbit.*

For myself when the children were younger I kept the teacher books separate and graded their papers with them. Now that they're older I allow them to keep the teacher books and grade their own papers. Of course we go over things together later on that morning. I keep a zippered binder with red, black, and blue pens, eraser, sharp pencils, some extra paper, and stickers. This is everything I might need while going over lessons. I'll explain more of this in the chapter on *Nesting*.

Look for interesting containers everywhere. Local stores all have cheap, nice-looking storage items. It is very important for everything to look nice and blend together. We all want to live in a house that looks and feels comforting. It is truly a blessing. So, really try to work on this. Below are some rules that will help keep everything in its place after all your hard work is done. If you and your family remember these rules and put them into action getting school finished each day will feel much easier and you'll feel much more in control.

1. The one touch rule. You can only touch something once before putting it away. **Hint. If it's in your hand you're touching it.**

2. Transition time. Pay attention when you're in between classes and duties. Use this time to put things back in order before attempting the next responsibility.

3. Habit. It's really just a matter of a good and efficient routine. If you've gotten into some bad habits, it time to change them into good ones. I tacked up a quote in the children's play room when they were young that read, "I always put my things away, that I might find them another day." These are words to live by.

4. Label. Labeling can help remind everyone exactly where something belongs, and where to put it.

5. <u>Re-evaluate</u>. You may notice that some of the places you thought would work aren't working very well after all. This is normal. Don't give up. Remember, if at first you don't succeed try, try again.

It is important to be flexible. I have my dishes back in the china cabinet now, and there is no longer a dresser in the living room, but there is a beautiful, antique buffet with school stuff inside.

Do yourself and your family a favor and get your things in order. You will be empowered by it. I promise. And when you need a protractor during geometry class you will know right where to find one.

"Order is never observed; it is disorder that attracts attention because it is awkward and intrusive"...

James B. Schafer

D = DUTIES

"The great person respects himself; he serves and helps, but is never slavish or servile. You cannot help your family by being a slave to them, or by doing things by right they should do for themselves."

Wallace Wattles

Every loving parent by nature wants to treat their children like royalty. But the royals of yesteryear would be shocked at the lack of knowledge our children have for protecting the family assets and keeping their home running smoothly. When Mom and Dad need a helping hand, children are just the ones to assist. If you start young enough they even like to help, and by the time they are in their tweens they'll know how to do almost all household chores. I am well aware that it is popular to allow children to be lazy and disrespectful. But just like the beehive hairdos of the sixties and early seventies it really isn't all that cool. Whenever I hear parents laughing and joking about how lazy their children are. I want to say, "Really? Is it something to laugh at?"

I believe that teaching children how to run a household and be responsible for chores is the original home economics class. Giving children duties actually boosts their self-esteem. It is a proven fact that self-confident people are the most powerful. Not only will giving children chores encourage confidence, but self-discipline as well. People who are self-disciplined are willing to work hard to get whatever it is they want, instead of hoping someone else will come along and do a difficult task for them. Education, as we are learning, is not all about academics.

When homeschooling, a family is home a lot more than if the children went to school and mom and dad both had jobs. That means that there is more food to prepare, more dishes to wash, more toys to pick up. You have to sweep more often, and the list goes on. Besides all those chores there are lessons to teach. Momma can become overwhelmed and overworked if she doesn't have help. She may even develop what I call "doorbell-aphobia." This means that when someone comes to the door she scrambles in a scared attempt to hide and stash the rubble lying about. Then answers the door with apologies about the state of her home, giving excuses as to why it looks like it does.

If your children don't have duties, homeschooling them is equal to a full time job away from home while others are at your house eating your food, dirtying your dishes, and generally messing up your home without supervision. You can't do it all. You need my *Duty Directory*. You can download the one made for our family for free off my website, www.laurahuber.com. Or you can make your own. It's easy.

Start by sitting in each room, looking everything over from top to bottom. Is there a ceiling fan that needs dusted on a regular basis? Now, work your way down, sconces, light fixtures, pictures. Write everything down that it will take to keep the room sparkling clean. Below is an example of a page in my *Duty Directory*.

LIVING ROOM:
Daily Tasks: *(use tally marks-should have 7 by end of week)*
_____ Straighten up. (Put everything back in its place. Items belonging to individuals can be placed on their beds, for them to put away—shoes next to bed)

_____ Shake rug.

_____ Sweep.

Weekly Tasks: *(just need one check mark)*

_____ Dust fan

_____ Get down cobwebs (on ceiling and candelabras-
be careful)

_____ Dust everything (couches, buffet, table) don't
 forget legs and bottoms

_____ Straighten under Dad's table

_____ Wash sliding glass doors

Monthly Tasks: *(performed only once a month when the listed person is
assigned to this room)*

_____ Sweep under couches-Keith

_____ Sweep under buffet-Elijah

_____ Sweep off top of armoire-Kristin

_____ Wipe off pictures-mom

*(Because there isn't a lot to do each day in the living room the person cleaning
the living room also takes care of cleaning the porch and car.)*

PORCH—daily

_____ Straighten

_____ Sweep porch and sidewalk

SUV—weekly

_____ Straighten back and throw away all trash

_____ Sweep and dust

Each child is given a page from the *Duty Directory* every week
that he or she is responsible for completing. Each week we switch.
I have only three children so I'm in on the rotation. Making it only
once a month when I must do a thorough cleaning of each room.
It's really easy once you have a system down. The children seem to
like it because—it's fair, and every day they know exactly what is
expected of them. When school is over and their jobs are finished

they have the rest of the day to spend as they wish. Lists will change and grow as do your children.

After showing your children how to perform each task correctly walk away, allowing him to see it through alone. If you're constantly stepping in saying things like, "No, that's not right." or "Here, let me do it." The child may hear it as, "You are too dumb and too slow." Remember that any housework completed is better than no housework completed.

Also, remember that children are just mini adults. Sometimes they get busy and overwhelmed, too. If this happens take the time to surprise them and do a few of their duties for them—just don't make it a habit.

"A weaken sense of responsibility does not weaken the fact of responsibility."
William J. Bennett

E = EXAMPLE

"Be the change you wish to see in the world. You can make the world a better place by starting at home."

Mohandas Gandhi

Be of noble character all you parents. Your children are watching every move you make, whether you are aware of it or not. One of my mom's favorite quotes is by Benjamin Franklin who said, "A good example is the best sermon." These are some powerful words, because we all know children learn what they live. It may be easier to talk the talk but, you really have to walk the walk.

If you don't want your child to do it—don't do it. If you don't want your child to say it—don't say it. If you want your child to act with dignity, integrity, and wisdom you will have to show them how in all situations. Even when they aren't around and they have no idea what you are doing, you have to set a good example, because people will treat your children in different ways depending on what they know about you. Long after you have done a good deed your children can still benefit. This has happened to me on more than one occasion.

Once when my husband's truck broke down on the highway, he needed someone to tow him home. Now, we all know how much those towing bills can be, especially if one must go far, as was this particular incident. Imagine my surprise when we went to pay the tow bill and the owner of the tow truck said, "For you it is free of charge." "Free?" I said, "I don't understand." "Yes, it's free. You see, when I was a young man, I was forced to file bankruptcy. It was horrible, no one in this small town believed in me anymore, no one that is except your father. I asked him to deliver some gravel, expecting him to be like everyone else that knew of my situation, and turn me down or demand payment upon delivery. I explained to him that I couldn't pay right away. He told me that it was okay, he trusted me for the money. Do you know what it means to have someone believe in you when no one else does? Well, it's something you never forget. That is why I insist that your tow bill is free."

I wasn't even six years old when this exchange took place between my father and the tow truck man, but over twenty years later my husband and I both benefited from my father's good example. Keep that in mind when you're tempted to lose your cool or not do the right thing.

On another occasion my children and I were at an antique tractor show. I saw some men who were squeezing the juice out of stalks of cane to make sorghum molasses. We started talking and found out that they actually bought the cane mill from my grandfather's brother—my great uncle. When I went to purchase some of their molasses they didn't charge me full price. I said, "I think there has been a mistake, this should be $8 not $4." "For you," the man said, "it will always be half price, because of the kindness and the patience your family showed us. They not only gave us a good price on the press, but also took the time to show us how to run it so we could start our business off much quicker. I was astonished that they didn't charge us, but was even more amazed that your nana made us a wonderful noontime meal. We'll never forget it."

The whole of the matter didn't hit me until we were walking away and my oldest son looked at me and said, "Wow, Mom, because of your family being nice, over thirty years later you're still benefiting from it." From that time on I realized how important it is to always do what is right and even go the extra mile. This incident made quite an impression on my children, too. Don't worry about getting paid back, eventually everything comes back.

How much better it is for me as person to have people praising my family and showing me the kindness that was shown to them by my parents, grandparents, and even my aunt and uncles.

Sometimes you have to be kind when you don't feel kind. Bite your tongue and smile at that nasty cashier or rude person. If you snap at people don't wonder why your kids do it, too. Sometimes you have to be patient when you feel like knocking someone's block off. Sometimes you have to swallow your pride and admit defeat or that you've made a mistake. Sometimes you have to do the exact opposite and stand up for yourself. Sometimes you have to be brave when you don't feel brave. This might be the hardest thing I've mentioned yet.

If you appear scared of storms, your children are more likely to be scared also. When you have a phobia it can be quite challenging to be brave. I personally am a little scared of heights. Of course, it seems all of our vacations involve some kind of a look-out tower high above the ground or a narrow rock pass that looking over the side can make me feel more than a little on edge. Sky lifts and zip lines are not the places you would expect to see a person with acrophobia. But can you imagine what I would be missing if I sat on the sidelines and waited for them to come back? Also, what kind of a message would I be sending?

Once I had to really fake being brave. One rather warm night, my husband got up and opened a window to freshen our room. It was dark and he didn't realize there wasn't a screen in the window. I kissed him as he left for work the next morning and went upstairs to make our bed. I picked up a pillow to find ... *(pardon me while I shiver and shake a bit here)* ... a big, black, hairy bat—with real fangs! Immediately, I threw the pillow back on top of the bat and called for our oldest son, who was only ten at the time. He is a sort of "Davy Crocket" kind of kid, so I hoped he could help. "Please, Keith, can you help Mom get this bat out? You are so brave." He gave me a look that showed as much fear as I felt. I swallowed hard and knew it was up to me. I had to show my little audience, now consisting of all three of our children, that Momma could take care of the problem. I grabbed my broom and dust pan and squeezed the bat between them. I gave it a toss out the same window it came in, but it didn't go back out. No. It somehow attached itself to the bottom of the open window; dangling there, clinging to the sash it mocked me, while a shivered. On my second attempt I used the dust pan to scrape it off and tried throwing it out again. I said a silent prayer of thanks as I watched it flying far, far away. The children cheered and I walked back downstairs a little taller, with my spine a little straighter, knowing that I was bigger than a bat in more ways than one.

If you can do something, it encourages your children that they can do it, too, no matter what it might be. My sister once told me that her boys told her that my kids believed I could do anything. To this day I'm sure it was because of the bat incident. But, if this sort of thing terrifies you I wouldn't suggest it. Call a neighbor or the fire department, and you'll still be a hero to your children if you don't freak out.

In his book, *Your Best Life Now*, Joel Osteen, tells a story of a dog whose back legs became paralyzed after being hit by a car. The dog learned to overcome this terrible injury by using her front legs and dragging the back ones along. Soon the dog gave birth to some of the cutest little puppies you've ever seen. After a while the owners of the dogs noticed that the puppies were also dragging their legs. They immediately took them to the vet, thinking that the puppies had been injured at the same time their mother was hurt. To everyone's shock and surprise the puppies' legs were fine. There wasn't a thing wrong with any of them. They were just mimicking their mother. Interesting story, huh?

One day when my daughter and a friend were playing house and pretending to be mommies, the way many little girls do, her friend suggested they lay the babies down and go outside for a smoke. Guess what her mother does?

How do you speak? To your children, to your spouse, to the neighbor down the street. Do you use proper English? Do you curse? Is your voice kind or harsh? How do you greet people? Can you look them in the eye and treat them all like they are important to you?

How do you dress? What kind of an example are you sending forth? There is a reason that police officers and business men and women dress the way they do. How would you feel about your banker if he was wearing sweatpants and a wife-beater tank top when you went in to ask for a loan? Our clothes send out subliminal messages that we're not always aware of. I do not suggest dressing like your local banker at home or in public, but I do think you should wear something every day that makes you feel good, is comfortable, and appropriate to the situation. In her book *Simple Abundance*, Sarah Ban Breathnach states that when our hair is in place and we like what we are wearing there is a direct co-relation to our days running smoothly. When our skirt is too tight, riding up our thighs and your doo goes flat, the day doesn't go quite as nice as we would like.

Confucius once said, "From the loving example of one family, a whole state may become loving; from the ambition and perseverance of one man, the whole state may be thrown into a rebellion. Such is the nature of influence ..." To set a good example at all times is a tall order. There will be days when you are not at your best. But on a daily basis try to look your best, be kind and brave, making wise decisions, listening to others, helping someone in need. Standing up for what is right. Your children are always watching.

"Example is the school of mankind, and they will learn at no other ..."

Edmund Burke

F = FUN FRIDAYS

"Most happiness is overlooked because it doesn't cost anything ..."

William Ogden

One of the many reasons I decided to homeschool was because I wanted to create lots of fun memories with my children. Everywhere I went, when my children were young, people would say to me, "Enjoy it while you can, they grow up so fast." I didn't want to be one of those parents who looked back on my kids' childhood with a yearning that we should've spent more time together. Now that they're ages, seventeen, sixteen, and fourteen, I look back with many fond memories, but to be quite honest, I still wish that I would've taken things a little less serious sometimes and stopped more often to pay closer attention to what they were saying, cherishing the short stubby dandelions they picked me so often, instead of smiling saying thanks, then thinking in the back of my mind, "what's for supper?"

At some point when the children weren't even in school yet, I decided to make some fun family rituals. One of the first things I put into place was that Friday night was pizza night. This took away the burden of meal planning for one night. Sometimes I would make the pizza completely from scratch; sometimes I would just "doctor up" a frozen one, and sometimes we would get "take out" and a movie. Everyone to this day still looks forward to pizza night. It is a time of unwinding; releasing the trials of the past week and at the same time looking forward to the weekend.

After we started homeschooling, the children I decided to make all day Friday, a fun day. But to make Friday a real fun day you must start on Monday. Make Mondays meaningful. Take it slow and steady like the famous fictitious turtle we all know and love. I like to keep things low key. I started this practice after reading, *Essene Book of Meditations and Blessings,* by Danaan Parry. Even though we consider ourselves modern day people we can still learn from a group of people living over 2,000 years ago, known as the Essenes, a cloistered sect living in the middle eastern desert. Some of their teachings tell us that John the Baptist may have been an Essene. Many people believe the Essenes deserve the credit for writing the Dead Sea Scrolls.

On Mondays the Essenes had a complete day of silence. Ooooh, doesn't that sound good to modern day mothers? Can you imagine a complete day of silence? Well, if you are surrounded by children this is not likely to occur, but you can slow things down on Mondays. You can try to speak in a quieter tone encouraging your children to do the same. You can think before you speak. One of my aspirations is to speak less and say more. I try to concentrate on doing this on Mondays. Do not listen to the radio or turn on the television on Mondays until much later in the day, if at all. Also, try staying away from the computer as much as possible, unless you are using it for lessons. Make Mondays meaningful by keeping things peaceful with slow determination and progress.

Meaningful Mondays make Teachful Tuesdays. This is a day to learn something new. Celebrate life; be excited about the day. The Essenes focused on their blessings on Tuesdays, taking long walks in nature, truly looking at the colors and truly smelling the earth using all their senses. I like to get a lot accomplished on

Tuesdays and sometimes can even pack in a few extra lessons with the kids.

Teachful Tuesdays make Wonderful Wednesdays. On Wednesdays the Essenes would wake up early to watch the sunrise and feel its warmth on their face. Doesn't that sound like a good way to start the day? Shamefully, I admit that personally I have only done this a time or two, but it really is a wonderful experience. Wednesdays can be wonderful whether you get up and soak up the sunrise or not. By working slow and steady on Monday, and teaching a few new and extra things on Tuesday, you feel like you've already accomplished something on Wednesday, instead of wondering where the week went. You're on course and ready to get something done.

Wonderful Wednesdays make Thankful Thursdays. Thursday was a bathing day for the Essenes. Imagine how good that must have felt to the people living in the hot, sanding desert, their bodies caked with sweat and dirt. They fully immersed themselves under clean water, washing away not only the dirt and grime of the past week, but all of their worries and mistakes as well. We can start our day out by showering off the week's previous trials, and tribulations, and by getting in another good day of teaching, helping and advising our school age children. I like to really clean my house good on this day and attempt to get the grass cut, too. So everyone can enjoy a three day weekend.

Finally, Thankful Thursdays make Fun Fridays. Fridays were a day of contemplation of the breath of life for the Essenes. For mothers homeschooling their children this is a day when we breathe in really deep, hold it, hold it, let it out slowly and say, "Aaaahhhh." Pat yourself on the back while admitting, "Job well done." Sid Caesar once said, "In between goals is a thing called life that has to be lived and enjoyed."

If the weather permits this is a good day to go to the zoo, go to the park, ride bikes together. Do something fun. Try out those science experiments that were suggested during the busy week. Complete an art project. Put in the DVD *School House Rock* and relive your youth. (Well maybe you're too young for that, but I'm not.) *School House Rock* will teach your kids the pre-amble to the constitution, multiplication tables, adjectives, verbs, and many other important subjects to tunes that will stick in their head forever. Play some fun educational games together. One of the main ways my children learned the Greek and Latin roots was by playing *Rummy Roots*. The makers of the game suggest playing it like Rummy—hence the name, but I suggest playing it like concentration. Shuffle well, place all cards face down and try to match the Greek or Latin root with the corresponding English word. Note to mothers: My children always beat me at this game, because their concentration level is much better than mine. In my defense I am helping them all and constantly reminding each child that chronos means time and para means beside. By the way, it comes with a cheat sheet, if your modern education failed you. Another fun game is *Great States*; this has all kinds of benefits for children learning state capitals, geography, and many other cool facts about our country. A link to purchase these and other games is provided on my website.

There are many, many other simple easy affordable ideas to do with your children. Once when mine were studying the adventurous Louis and Clark expedition, I took them canoeing—down the river—not up like the courageous discoverers. Be creative allow your kids to help with these ideas to make your Fridays Fun. The famous Dale Carnegie tells us, "People rarely succeed unless they have fun in what they are doing." We all want our children to succeed, so make sure you incorporate some fun things for your family to enjoy together. If you have trouble trying to come up with fun ideas, in my book, *The Life Planner,* I give four or more suggestions each month based on the seasons of the year. Try reading Sarah Ban Breathnach's, *Simple Abundance* and *Mrs.*

Sharp's Traditions. In these books you will find numerous suggestions for some free old-fashioned fun.

"I never did a day's work in my life. It was all fun."

Thomas A. Edison

G = GOALS

"You have to think anyway, so why not think big?"

Donald Trump

T.S. Elliot tells us that, "If you haven't the strength to impose your own terms on life, you must accept the terms it offers you." Ouch! That hurts a bit, doesn't it? In other words, if we don't make some goals, we will be swept away by the currant of life. Up the proverbial creek without a paddle. Can you imagine how different your life might be today if when you were in school you would have been taught the importance of goal setting and how to attain them? What if each year of school you worked on goals that really mattered to you, instead of finishing that 500 word essay about why baking soda and vinegar create a fizz. Would you, could you, now be living a life of luxury … the life dreams are made of? I'm not saying it isn't important to study all the primary subjects. Achieving most goals will be easier if you know how to calculate, read, and write—not to mention learning from the great masters of the past—but Albert Einstein says, "Perfection of means and confusion of goals seem to characterize our age." And I think he's on to something.

Everybody wants their children to attain the life of their dreams, but do we ever take the time to really show them how this can be done? Do we really believe it can be done? When my youngest son was about five I asked him what he wanted to be. He replied, "An undercover cowboy." It's a little hard to know how to achieve that goal, especially without a horse and saddle. "Goals are simply tools to focus your energy in positive directions, they can be changed as your priorities change, new ones added, and others dropped." O. Carl Simonton tells us. The important thing is to have goals to work towards. Elijah doesn't want to be an undercover cowboy anymore, but it was a fun goal for him to have when he was five.

Every year before school starts, I make a rough sketch of things I would like to teach our children and books I would like to read with them. Then I ask each child what he or she would like to accomplish and learn. The steps listed below are invaluable to achieving your goals, because if you don't have a plan on how to reach your goals—goals become nothing more than wishes.

1. Decide what it is you really want and when you want it.
2. Determine what it is you will do to attain it.
3. Write down the answers to number 1 and 2 on a sturdy piece of paper. This is very important because you need to look at your goals each day, morning, noon and night. Rolf Smith tells us that, "The problem with making mental notes is that the ink fades very rapidly."
4. Say, **"NO!"** to naysayers. Many people will try to discourage you and your children when they hear your lofty goals. Let most advice go in one ear and out the other, unless the person giving the advice happens to be very successful. Then you may want to pay attention. Otherwise look at the person and say, **to yourself**, "How's that working for you?"

5. Put it in God's hands and believe you will receive your desire. If you don't believe in it you probably won't achieve it, no matter what it is. Even Jesus said, "Believe that you shall receive and you shall receive."

6. Take action. Whatever you truly want in life should not be left to chance; you must begin achieving your goals by taking action. The founder of the Atari game, Nolan Bushnell believes, "Everyone who has ever taken a shower has had an idea. It's the person who gets out of the shower, dries off, and does something about it that makes a difference.

Goals will give you and your children a reason to get up, get dressed, and get going in the morning. They are an incentive to keep you motivated all day. Harvey Mackay, an author and speaker, says, "Goals tend to tap the deeper resources and draw the best of life." Don't you want to draw the best of life and don't you want to show your children how to do it too?

The beginning quote by Donald Trump says we should think big, but you may want to start small. In my book, *The Life Planner*, I suggest starting out by writing down only five things you want to accomplish each day. If you get more finished that's a bonus. I also suggest writing a goal for each week, each month, and an ultimate goal for the year. If these goals are lofty then chunk them down into bite size pieces. We've all heard the old saying about how to eat an elephant—one bite at a time. Setting goals keeps your mind focused on what is really important to you in life. Start today by writing down some goals. Then encourage your children to do the same. Have a small celebration when someone in the family achieves a goal he or she has been working on. Give lots and lots of praise. Soon you will be living the life you thought possible only in your dreams. And your children will have a major head start in determining their course for life.

The famous basketball player Larry Bird tells us, "A winner is someone who recognizes his God-given talents, works his tail off to develop them into skills, and uses these skills to accomplish his goals." Your children each have some kind of special talent. Hone in on these skills when helping them set and achieve goals. It will make their life a lot more fun, and yours, too.

"If you have built castles in the air, your work need not be lost; that is where they should be. Now put the foundations under them."

Henry David Thoreau, Walden

H = HEART'S DESIRE

"There is no scarcity of opportunity to make a living at what you love, there's only scarcity of resolve to make it happen."

Wayne Dyer

I think my oldest son knew from birth what he wanted to do in life ... be a farmer. My husband and I are not farmers, my father is a hobby farmer, we are surrounded by farms and farmers, but it is not something we tried to implement in his being. It is just something he has always wanted to do. We knew something was up on his first birthday. My mother gave him a tractor that looked just like his grandpa's. Our son, who is normally quiet and easy-going, became possessive and aggressive, allowing no one to touch the beloved tractor. From then on his love of farming grew.

When he was eight or nine he became the star quarterback of the local county football team. After one particular game the boys on his team were shouting, "Keith! Keith! Keith!" Then they asked him to go to the bowling alley and celebrate their latest victory. He graciously declined by saying, "No, thanks. I want to go home and help the farmers haul manure." I was appalled by his answer and wanted to celebrate with the other parents and the kids on his team. Not one to get caught up in glory, Keith knew his heart's desire, and stayed the course. Me a little more than worried at the time that he wasn't like all the other boys.

But, by the age of sixteen, he had saved over ... are you ready for this ... ten thousand dollars! He did this completely on his own; doing not much more than part time work, for farmers who live near us. Because he enjoys working on farms and is a natural at it, he has become a well-sought-after hired hand. One day, while at my parents' home, my mother watched and listened to him in amazement on his cell phone, arranging his plans for his next day of work. "He's running a business," she commented in an astonished voice. Yes, in a way he does run his own business. Working steady for one farmer, then arranging his day so he can bush hog, mow grass, or move sows for other farmers. This is without any assistance from anyone. Sometimes when he comes home after a long day of hard work, I ask him, "Do you really want to do this? You know you don't have to work this hard." His reply, "Mom, it's fun to me." How can a mother argue with that?

What I'm trying to say is that farming may or may not be the field I would have chosen for him. But it is the field he was made for. Many parents have dreams of their children going to college, becoming the winner of the Nobel Peace Prize, or president of the United States of America. Your child on the other hand, may have other ideas. Make sure you want *their* heart's desire for them, and not *your* heart's desire for them. Even if your child is a wiz when it comes to working algebra problems, it doesn't mean he will be a mathematician. Every individual must be able to listen to the guidance within. God gave us feelings to use as a barometer of the self. Every second your feelings are pointing you in the right direction if you pay attention to them. Pay attention to what your children love doing. Pay attention to what you love doing. If you're doing something and get totally wrapped up in it, losing all track of time, because you're enjoying yourself so much, it's probably what you were created to do. It's your heart's desire.

Teach your children to pay close attention to those silent nudgings and feelings, never suppressing them. This doesn't mean if they're afraid of water, you don't teach them how to swim. No. You talk with them trying to find out why they are afraid of the water—then teach them how to swim. It may open up a whole new world or even a new heart's desire for them. Be careful, kids can be shifty, and your own words can and will be used against you, when teaching children to go for their heart's desire. So be on guard, when you start teaching this lesson. Once I wrote an article for *Home Education Magazine.* In the article I explained how my oldest son didn't think he needed to learn proper grammar, because "a farmer wouldn't ever need it." (*You can read the article on my website.*) I created a scenario with him. Him being the employer, me being interviewed with a couple of different levels of grammar skills. In the end he admitted that it was important to speak with proper grammar.

Achibald MacLeish, a lawyer and an American poet, tells us that, "The crisis of our time, as we are beginning slowly and painfully to perceive, is a crisis not of the hands but of the hearts…" So often as parents we are so focused on what we think is best for our child, forgetting about the true nature of the child himself. Take a long, hard look at what you are doing this year in school. Inventor of the first digital calculator, mathematician and physicist, Blaise Pascal, said, "The heart has its argument with which the logic of the mind is not acquainted …" Are you cramming stuff down your kid's throat just because someone in the government thought it would be a good idea for every single school age student to learn to read, write, or complete a year of algebra at a certain age? If so you may want to think again about why and what you are teaching your children, remembering to use some of your own authority. If you break a child's heart—you also break his spirit. Never forget that each person learns and develops at different times and stages in their life. Each and every child has his own talents and gifts that he brings into this world.

One of the best ways to get children (and yourself, too) in touch with their true heart's desire is to create a Discovery Journal. A discovery journal is much different than a regular journal, which we will discuss later. A discovery journal taps the imagination of your heart. To create one you will need:

1. A notebook (any notebook or scrap book will do, but it is important for it to have a good binding because you will be looking through it often.)

2. A pile of old magazines with lots of pictures—including something for everyone's interests.

3. A scissors.

4. A glue stick.

I like to save working in the discovering journal for Fridays, mostly cold or rainy winter Fridays. All you do is cut out things that catch your eye, in no particular order and no regard for cost. Cut out words, sentences, pictures, even whole pages. If you do this with your children you will learn things about yourself and your children that you never would have imagined before. It is a quite enjoyable way to start making plans, setting goals, and mapping the future you would like to see take shape.

"It is more fatal to neglect the heart than the head."

Theodore Parker

I = IMAGINATION

"Imagination is more important than knowledge. For knowledge is limited to all we know and understand. While imagination embraces the entire world."

Albert Einstein

If Albert Einstein, one of the most famous scientists of our time, thinks imagination is more important than knowledge we better reconsider how all of our children are being taught, looking more closely into the benefits the imagination can bring to them.

Today people tend to think that children need to have something planned for them every minute of the day. Because of this children can go all through life never tapping into their greatest resource—their imagination. Between computer games, watching television, dancing lessons, softball practice, and volley ball camp a young girl of age eight might not get the time she needs during the summer to tap into her fabulous imagination just waiting to be discovered. I find that many parents today, with the best interest of the children in mind, over schedule and over stimulate their kids. Running to and fro, back and forth, giving children little time to just be.

To just be: a firefighter, an airplane pilot, a farmer, a mommy, a daddy, a cowboy, a cowgirl, an investigator, a civil war hero, a nurse, a monkey, a dog, a cat, a super hero ... the list goes on unceasingly, yet how many kids today ever get the chance to discover the magnificent things their imagination can do or the many places it can take them. Joseph Chilton Pearce says, "Play is the only way the highest intelligence of humankind can unfold."

If your kids are not ones to play on their own and do not show signs of a vivid imaginations you will have to show them how to do it at first. Have you ever seen the old movie, *A Miracle on 34th Street?* In it Chris Cringle shows a young girl who has never used her imagination what it might like to be a monkey. The girl finds that it is quite fun to use her imagination, and your kids will too. Show them how by taking about fifteen minutes to play and then suggest some ideas for them to do on their own. Use this quote by Dr. Seuss to help get them going in the right direction, "Think left and think right and think low and think high. Oh, the thinks you can think up if you only try!" Then let the kids take over. Soon they will come to you with tales of how they slayed a dragon and saved a maiden from certain death.

Kay Redfield Jamison, professor of psychiatry, goes so far as to say, "Play is not a luxury it is a necessity." When children are playing they are in charge of their own world and the problems that may exist there. They can solve what might be an imaginative adult problem in an environment that they control by using a solution that they themselves have come up with. This in turn will give them the confidence and common sense many young adults are lacking today.

Can you imagine what our world would be like today if the Wright brothers didn't have the time to use their imagination? A flying machine is not something the logical mind could conceive. John Scully, a business executive says, "The future belongs to those who see possibilities before they become obvious." Anyone who ever accomplishes anything must first spend a certain amount of time daydreaming, desiring, and imagining what it is he or she wants to be, have, or do. If you can't see it in your imagination how can it ever come to be? I agree fully with Napoleon Hill when he wrote in his book, *Think and Grow Rich*, "The practical dreamers have always been and always will be the pattern-makers of civilization ... Every great leader from the dawn of time was a dreamer. Dreams are not born of indifference, laziness or lack of ambition."

Our children could play trucks and Barbie dolls for hours, even days. In the summer they would play in their large, sprawling sand pile until the sun went down. Creating roads and bridges, homes and businesses. I always loved to watch them without them noticing me. Watching them sort of brought out the endless imagination in myself, and brought me back to the lazy days of my own childhood.

One of my favorite movies is *Toy Story*. Probably because many of the toys were things that I grew up playing with. I always loved pretending that my toys had feelings and lives like they do in that movie. I think it is important for children to treat their toys with love and respect because I have noticed a direct co-relation in some children who destroy their toys and turn around to only disrespect real people. Making children take care of the things they use to stimulate their childhood imagination can only aid them in real life, helping them to care for more valuable things they may own or care about in the future.

When I look back to when my children were younger, the electronic toys were fun for a while, but the toys that required imagination were the ones that held their attention the longest. My daughter received her first *American Girl* baby doll when she was six years old. From that day on her collection grew. She and her little friends from the neighborhood played with those things every day until they were almost teenagers.

On our one acre plot of land and inside our two thousand square foot house we have had weddings, county fairs, 1,000 acre farms, Indian villages, kittens dressed in baby clothes, horses that were really bicycles, sand castles, floods, forests and much more. When encouraging imagination one must not get too picky about the rules of the house. So take heed from an anonymous tip, "Imagination has the capability to choose pain and disorder in the same measure as it does goodness and order ..." Don't worry if your house is in disarray from children using their imagination, everyone can help at the end of the day putting everything back in order.

"Trust that little voice in your head that says, 'Wouldn't it be interesting if ...' and then do it."

Duane Michals

J = JOURNALING

"The pen is mightier than the sword."

Edward Bulwer

I have always been a bit of a rebel when it comes to education. As for reports and lengthy papers, I have assigned a very minimal amount. I do however; strongly believe in journaling <u>every single day of school</u>. The journal works as a tool in many ways:

1. It promotes creative writing.
2. It is a time to practice handwriting
3. It can be used as a grammatical tutorial.
4. It can be used to hone spelling skills.
5. It can be used to promote proper punctuation.
6. It is a history book of the life of your child.

"Each thought that is welcomed and recorded, is a nest egg by the side of which more will be laid." Henry David Thoreau tells us. As your children grow they will enjoy looking back at the awkward entries they scratched down in their earlier years. "Oh, yeah! Remember when we went to the Civil War Re-enactment?" or "I'd almost forgot about when Eli learned to ride his bike and put that deep scratch in the door of your Suburban, Mom." It is all recorded. But the best part is that when they are writing in their journal most of the time they don't realize it is a school assignment.

Don't expect too much from the content of their journals at first. Many times all my boys would write about was how the game went the night before. That is okay. This is just to get them to practice writing without being forced. (Although at times force may be needed.)

There are many different types of journals. Children will be more apt to enjoy writing in them if they pick one out. **Note. Make sure the journal has lines.** This is really the only requirement for me. We have found beautiful journals at Christian book stores, but we have also used plain, old, spiral-bound notebooks with cute kittens and puppies on the front cover found at your local department store. You could also buy a plain notebook, glue cardstock to the front of it and have the children decorate their own—especially if you're running short of art projects for the month.

I began using journaling as a helpful tool as soon as my children could write easily on basic notebook paper. This was usually around the second or third grade. Always remember every child is different and what worked good for my children at the age of eight may work for yours at a much earlier or older age, so adjust to the individual child.

When you start using the journal explain to your children that this is a journal for school and it is different from a personal diary. Mom will be looking at the work recorded in the school journal and using errors and mistakes to make them a better writer, while enhancing grammar and spelling skills also. If your child wants to keep a private journal this is done separately from school time and his privacy is respected unless an emergency situation arises.

Some things to keep in mind when using the journal tool:

1. Always make the children write the date. This will help them learn and spell the days of the week and months of

the year. When children are younger write out the date for them on a chalkboard, dry erase board, or even just an index card. Example. Wednesday, October 24, 2011.

2. If the children complain that they have nothing new to write about give them some suggestions. Possibilities are endless. Remind them of something like, "What about the pretty rainbow we saw after yesterday's storm?" or "What if you wrote about how Grandpa made you that necklace out of a rock with a hole in it?" Kids tend to forget about all the cool stuff that happened the day before.

3. Encourage them to start their school work or end their school work with the journal so it becomes a habit pattern in their school routine.

4. After school work is finished sit down together and read the entry. Always start off correcting mistakes with kind words. "This is a really good journal entry. I can tell you worked hard on it."

5. Explain what the child did wrong in an encouraging way. "Whenever you end a sentence be sure to use a punctuation mark." Now is a good time to reinforce the punctuation lesson given just minutes before. "Remember how if it is a command or statement it ends with a period but if it is a question then we need …" This can get more challenging as children get older, but no worries— sometimes you will be learning right along with them.

6. **Always** give the child a sticker. I don't care if they are in twelfth grade; everyone likes to feel like he or she did a good job. Even if they don't deserve praise try to find something in the journal entry that they did right.

"Journal writing is a voyage to the interior"

Christina Baldwin

K = KINDNESS

"Treat everyone as if they each had a sign around their neck that said, 'make me feel important.'"

Mary Kay Ash

Kindness encourages and inspires. Kindness makes everything run smoother. In his book, *The Science of Getting Rich*, Wallace Wattles tells us to, "Let your attitude in business, politics, in neighborhood affairs, and in your own home be expressions of the best thoughts you can think. Let your manner toward all men and women great and small, and especially to your own family circle, always be the most kind, gracious, and courteous you can picture in your imagination."

Unfortunately, most of the time it is the ones we love and care about the most that don't receive the kindness they so desperately want and deserve. I'm not sure why many of us are kinder to strangers or neighbors than we are to our own loved ones. Isn't it interesting that Mr. Wattles tells us especially to be kind in our own family circle? If only kindness could be kept in a jar and brought out whenever we needed it, every day would run a lot smoother, because children, spouses, siblings, and parents can get on our nerves faster than the strangers at the grocery store. Because we know they'll always love us—no matter what—we tend to allow ourselves our worst behavior when around those precious people in our lives. Sad isn't it?

Have you ever thought of the effect a kind or unkind word has on the world. It is like throwing a small pebble into still water; the ripples tend to spread to circles more than a thousand times the circumference of the stone. My father once pointed out to me, when I was a teenager, how terrible he thought it was the way some parents talked about their kids. Hearing so many parents say things like, "It's a good thing God didn't give us teenagers to start out with, or no one would ever have kids." I just took it for granted that they had a point. After he stated out how detrimental that was to the child who happened to be standing there listening, I realized the significance of his words and was very glad he didn't feel that way about his own teenagers. It made me want to be a good person because I knew how much my parents loved me.

When my children were young there were many people who would comment on how cute they were; then followed the statement by saying, "Just wait until they're teenagers—then they're not so cute. You'll want to send them back." I've had so many conversations with parents that start out like this, "Hi Mrs. Smith, how are things going?" and she answers, "Terrible, these kids are brats!" Really? I wonder why they're brats? Have so many parents forgotten the golden rule: "Do unto others as you would have others do unto you." Maybe parents just don't realize the affect words have over a child or temporarily forget about the child's feelings. Mother Teresa, one of the kindest souls to ever live, gave us this advice, "Kind words can be short and easy to speak, but their echoes are truly endless."

Up until the 17th century everyone believed that raw meat gave life to maggots. Then a scientist named, Francesco Redi, disproved the theory that maggots spontaneously came to life from raw meat. The experiments he performed caused him to come up with a new theory that: Life begets life. I believe that kindness begets kindness, and I ask you to do your own experimenting to prove me right. Try putting on your best smile and thinking of the above quote by Mary Kay Ash that everyone is wearing a sign around his or her neck saying, "Make me feel important." Then notice the rippling effect it has on everyone's life and especially your own. Life is like a boomerang and whatever you throw out there will automatically come back to you. So if you want kindness—be kind. My father told me that whenever you throw dirt you lose ground.

The first person to start being kind to is yourself. Do I need to repeat this? Start by being kind to yourself. (*We will discuss more in the chapter titled, Me Time.*) This may be a new concept for you because many women believe their role in life is to be a martyr, giving and doing for everyone else. But it is much easier to do for everyone else if you're kind to yourself first. The tone of your voice will be more pleasant, and you will have more patience. You will be more willing to laugh and have fun if you're not feeling overwhelmed and over-worked. If you are anxious and stressed it's going to be really tough to be kind. Take it from someone who knows all too well. I'm not proud of the way I act and talk to my loved ones when I don't take time to be kind to myself by planning ahead or saying "no" to something that could cause me to be overwhelmed. When I am running on empty or running behind schedule, and worrying about being on time, that's when I am most irritable. I bet you are too. Little things that normally wouldn't matter can grate on your nerves until you completely snap and lash out at people with the most important feelings of all—your loved ones.

Some parents allow their children to fight and argue. I can take very little of this. I want my children to get along with each other and be kind. Knowing that when differences come up, they can be settled in a different way than arguing or fighting. One day when our two older children were bickering back and forth I called a neighbor and trusted friend. "What should I do to keep Keith and Kristin from fighting?" She answered, "I never allowed my children to fight. Whenever they did I made them sit on the couch and hold hands." I replied, "Okay, I'll try that." Many times I made my children hold hands. Once I even made them hold hands in public. Even my strict husband thought this was a little cruel, but they never ever had another argument in public again. Sometimes they had to hold onto both hands and look their opponent in the eye. All the while with me saying things like, "Aren't you thankful for your brother or sister?" Sometimes they would squeeze the daylights out of each other's hands until it seemed as if someone's fingers would fall off, but eventually they calmed down. That's when I would make them look at each other and say, "I'm sorry for … and I'm glad you're my brother/sister." I usually make everyone hug, even the people not involved, because any fight affects the whole family. If the day has taken on a tone or habit of saying not so kind things, I sit everyone in a circle, and make each person say three kind things to everyone sitting there—no repeats. I usually get the procedure started by saying three nice things about each of them like: "Kristin, you have been very helpful with the housework lately. I was thrilled to see how well you did on your math test. Thank you for helping Elijah feed his animals this morning." This gives the children a chance to come up with their own nice things about the rest of us. It always makes things better and everyone lightens up. Because it's true, all anyone wants is to feel loved and important.

Be very careful when trying to get your children to strive to become better. Our good intentions can sound a lot different then what is meant. An innocent incentive may sound a lot different to a child. "You really need to be more outgoing so you have more friends." Could sound like, "You're not socially acceptable." A good way to give kind well-meaning or much needed advice that is readily acceptable is to start out by praising the child with kind words, or by saying something like, "When I was younger it was so hard for me to make friends. I know if I could have only been friendlier and less shy I would have had more fun." That way the comment is directed away from the child's personal disposition.

I always try to make sure that everyone goes to bed happy and smiling. There is an old saying given to us by St. Paul in the book of Ephesians, "Never let the sun set on your anger." Now when the children are leaving for work or going out with friends I try to instill the same concept; that way returning home is much more inviting. I always tell them I love them and give them a kiss or hug and say have a good day or have fun. Many times I even do this in front of their friends. I am never mushy or gushy; it is always said with feeling and depth in a matter-of-fact way. The kids always hug me back and most of the time they say I love you, too. Sometimes even their friends come up to me for a hug. Kids like kindness. Kids want kindness. Kids need kindness. No matter if you're correcting a paper, disciplining a child," or waving goodbye. Cultivate kindness in your family circle until it naturally spills over to those outside your tight-knit group. We'll have a happier world because of it.

"To be kind is to live with grace, dignity, and elegance. It means taking an interest in life and caring about it enough to make it better for you and others."
                                                            Sonia Choquette

L = LISTENING AND LOVE
OF LEARNING

LISTENING

"The ear of the leader must ring with the voices of the people."

Woodrow Wilson

Is there anyone on this earth who hasn't felt a bit disheartened when he or she had something important to say and no one would listen? We all have had our bouts with people not hearing us. I remember when I was a child my mother would sometimes say, "I *feel* like I'm talking to the wall." I'm certain this always came after she had told us ten times to help with the chores. As I child I didn't understand what she meant. I remember thinking to myself, "Why don't you just stop talking then?" But like everything else she did or said, when I became a mother myself, these words took on a whole new meaning. As mothers we wonder sometimes if our children are hearing anything we say. I can guarantee they are hearing everything you want them to hear and then some. I bet my mother never knew I heard her saying she felt like she was talking to the wall until she read this book. Hank Ketcham, puts it this way, "Just because I didn't do what you told me doesn't mean I wasn't listening to you!" We know how important it is as adults to have someone to listen to us, so you can bet your children feel the same way.

Sometimes we cast off a child's ideas or stories as if they were nothing more than an insignificant piece of lint on our clothing. It is more important to listen to what your child is trying to tell you than it is for you to teach them to read. You can learn more by listening to your child than any book on child psychology could ever teach you about raising children. Take time to hear what it is they truly want or need. Philip Stanhope, Earl of Chesterfield once said, "Many a man would rather you heard his story than granted his request." Just because you listen to what your children are saying doesn't mean you have to agree with them or grant their request. John Bryan tells us, "You have to be willing sometimes to listen to some remarkable bad opinions. Because if you say to someone, 'That is the silliest thing I ever heard; get out of here.' then you'll never get anything out of that person again, and you might as well have a puppet on a string or a robot." The last things we want our children to be are puppets and robots. We want them to be independent thinkers. We can encourage this just by listening to what they have to say.

What would you do or say if your eighteen-year-old daughter, a straight A student, came up to you and said, "Mom and Dad I've decided I'm not going to college. I want to be one of those people who run the rides for the kids at county fairs." Would your first instinct be to suck in your breath, with shocked eyes and a rather horrified look on your face, blurting out, "You have got to be kidding?" or, would you calmly say something like, "Oh, really? How did you come up with that decision?" The child may answer, "Well, I think it would be fun going to different places each week and making little kids happy." You then come back with, "That's really great that you want to travel and make little kids happy, but do you think you would like the living conditions? Why don't you get online and check things out a little more. Maybe you could do some internet searching on traveling and working with children, just so you know all your options." Chances are your daughter will do just that if she's interested. And chances are she will make the right decision from some easy-going guidance from you. Guidance she doesn't even realize you are giving. Remember the words of Frank Crane, "Teaching is lighting a lamp and not filling a bucket ..." By remaining calm and asking questions you're putting the child's future back in her hands, yet still gently leading her to her heart's desire.

"Listening is a magnetic and strange thing, a creative force. The friends who listen to us are the ones we move toward. When we are listened to it creates us, makes us unfold and expand."

Karl Menninger

LOVE OF LEARNING

"The best teacher is the one who suggests rather than dogmatizes, and inspires his listener with the wish to teach himself ..."

Edward Bulwer Lytton

By listening closely to your children you can create a love of learning. By creating in your child a love of learning you are giving the child all the tools he needs to become a successful adult. You may question this last statement. *All the tools he needs to become a successful adult?* Yes, by creating a love of learning the child will teach himself about anything he is interested in. During the journey of learning about the things we love we also learn many other fascinating facts that have nothing to do with the chosen subject. For example, if your twelve-year-old daughter wants to learn about how World War II began, she may pick up some interesting information about the Jewish religion, world history, German language and customs, geography and more. From there the child may decide to learn more about Russia or Denmark. The possibilities are interminable. If your eight-year-old son wants to become a policeman, take him to your local police department to meet some of the men and women who work there. Make sure you call ahead of time to schedule the visit. Don't inundate the child with nothing but police work, it can be a very scary job. At the age of eight, all he needs to know are the good things about being a police officer. This is the perfect time to introduce some other important jobs people do in order to keep us safe or serve the general public. Go to the library and get some picture books about different kinds of public service jobs. Now would be a good time to take him to the fire department, post office, park service, etc.

When I was in school I absolutely HATED reading class. I loved to read, but found the chosen reading material uninteresting and shallow. If your child hates to read this is a major red flag that something needs to change—immediately! Because by reading you can teach yourself almost anything. Try to figure out why the child doesn't enjoy reading. Is the reading material too hard? Is it uninteresting to the student? Are you making the child read much longer than his mind can handle at one time? These are vital questions that must be addressed.

Once my children could start reading chapter books, I allowed them to pick and choose their own reading material. Of course I supervise whether or not it is morally and age appropriate. Every single day I read aloud with all my children, even though they are in high school now. This is a fun way to spend time with them and be involved in something together. I read a paragraph then the child I'm working with reads a paragraph. They have learned how to read out loud with feeling and emotion by doing this. **Note. Some kids will naturally do better than others.** Remember, God has bestowed special gifts for each and every child. Accept your children for the wonderful people they were created to be, and help them refine their gifts by creating a love of learning.

In the beginning it was a most challenging task teaching my youngest son Elijah to read. When he was little it was hard for me to stay awake while I listened to him read aloud. I thought that he must hate reading as much as he struggled with it. I voiced my opinion to my mother one day, "Elijah, hates reading." He overheard me and piped up and said, "MOM! I love reading. Why did you say that?" Thank God I had him reading books he was interested in.

I really didn't realize that there was a major problem until he was in the fourth grade. This is about the time dyslexia usually rears its stubborn head. My older two children were reading at a much faster pace and much harder material than he was at that age. I noticed that he was still struggling with b's and d's, m's and w's and words like saw and was (*saw is was spelled backwards*). I went to a seminar on dyslexia and learned how to teach him much better. I also realized at this seminar that he had dyscalculia. I had never heard of this before. Dyscalculia is to math class what dyslexia is to reading class. A person with dyscalculia has trouble calculating numbers. I never thought it possible when he was in sixth grade, but by going slowing at his desired pace we created a love of learning, and by the time Elijah was in eighth grade he was reading really well and actually got an A in his pre-algebra class. He can retain anything and is a really smart student. My guess is that his IQ is much higher than anyone in our family. If I had gone on doing the same things I had done with my older children I do not believe he would be as far ahead as his is now. Imagine that, by going at a slower pace he actually learned faster. *(Go to my website to receive free information on how to help a child with dyslexia or dyscalculia.)*

There is no such thing as the "average student." That is why so many kids do better with one-on-one attention. Albert Einstein once said that, "It is nothing short of a miracle that the modern methods of instruction have not yet entirely strangled the holy curiosity of inquiry ..." One of the most wonderful things about homeschooling is the parent can tailor the school days to the best interest of each child. Susie down the street may be learning a foreign language in ninth grade, but that doesn't mean your ninth grader has to do the same. Keeping up on what other children are doing is one thing. Making the child do what everyone else is doing will not create a love of learning.

One regret I have about my early homeschooling days is that I was so intent on teaching my little kindergarten son phonics and math, I didn't focus on what he was interested in. We had the neatest science book and he loved it. It could have been a lot more fun and enjoyable if we would've worked more in that and less on some of the other subjects. It's too late for me to go back and enjoy that science book with him, but it's not too late for you to learn from my mistakes. Although, I did find a really cool science book last year—that he loved!

Children need to be exposed to many different things just to graduate. It is very important to make sure you know exactly what it is that your state requires. If your child is enrolled in a homeschool academy, they may have different requirements than your state, but meeting those is all your child needs to receive his diploma. Just as important as meeting requirements for a diploma is making sure and taking time to find out exactly what it is your child wants to learn and is interested in. Dwelling mostly on the subjects your child loves and enjoys and giving only the amount of attention needed on all the others, will give the child a well-rounded education and create in him a love of learning. Cultivate and nurture the gifts your children have been blessed with and they will bless you by being eager students, and looking forward to school each day. Isn't that every mother's dream?

"The teacher, however great, can never give his knowledge to the pupils ... although ... he can kindle the light if the oil is in the lamp ..."

Hazrat Inayat Khan

M = ME TIME

"Self- love my liege, is not so vile a sin as self-neglecting."

William Shakespeare

Most mothers don't know the meaning of, "me time," unless it pertains to someone else in the family. Creating some down time for yourself is vital to you as well as your family. The first time one of my dear friends suggested this to me I scoffed at her saying, "That is completely impossible. There is no way I could begin to fit time into my day just for me. Everyone always needs something and there is always something that needs to be done." She suggested I read, *Simple Abundance* by Sarah Ban Breathnach. A copy lay upon my shelf for weeks untouched. Then I became pregnant with our fourth child. During this time I became very ill and was on bed rest for weeks. I watched as the cobwebs taunted me and the dust bunnies laughed in my face. Funny how if we are forced into submission we can take time for ourselves and relax. If a doctor tells you to take some me-time it's okay, otherwise it feels like a guilty pleasure. I decided to start reading *Simple Abundance*, after all, I couldn't do anything else. Its pages brought me peace and the realization that I had been running my life backward. In the forward Ms. Ban Breathnach chose to quote Margaret Young, *"Often people attempt to live their lives backwards: they try to have more things, or more money, in order to do more of what they want so that they will be happier. The way it actually works is the reverse. You must first be who your really are, then do what you need to do, in order to have what you want."*

Even though I wasn't going to a job every day to make more money to have more things, I was doing something similar, making sure that the grass was mowed, the house was cleaned, the checkbook balanced, groceries bought, supper on the table, laundry finished, gardens weeded, etc. I thought after I got all these chores finished I could start enjoying my family and my life. My children were ages seven, five, and three. My husband worked long hard hours so I didn't think he should have to help with anything. I was slowing becoming a suffering saint and a self-inflicted martyr. After being on bed rest for a while my body slowly started healing, but a fourth child was not meant to be and I suffered a miscarriage. I was devastated. I was already in the beginning of my fourth month— thought I was out of the woods—so to speak. I blamed myself, like so many women do. There were things I did and said that seemed to aid in the miscarriage. Because I had such a bad cold, I coughed and coughed pulling a back muscle. I put a heating pad on my back to ease the pain, and someone told me that may have caused the miscarriage. I had questioned God when I became pregnant and said something to the effect if he wanted me to keep homeschooling he better do something because, I was too busy for another child. I remember coming home from the hospital after the miscarriage, and waking up in the middle of the night, and for a brief sleep-induced moment searching for the baby making sure it was still breathing. But there was no baby this time. I felt so guilty for being so busy. Everything that used to seem important was no longer that important.

I dove into the pages of *Simple Abundance*, and its soothing suggestions saved me from myself. I learned to love myself. Find myself. Nurture myself. I learned about what I really loved to do. I started to take time in the morning after my husband left to read and relax, knowing that after the kids woke up there would be no more "me time." But that was okay. All I needed was an hour or so in the morning and I was good to go.

Try starting out each new day with a piping hot mug of peppermint tea. If coffee gets you going, than stick with it. It's fun to get comfortable on the sofa, surrounding yourself with inspiring books, and wonderful magazines, to get in touch with your higher self. This is also a good time to pray, meditate, and write in a journal. You will find things out about yourself that you never knew before. You may discover that you would someday like to live in a log cabin on top of a mountain. Or maybe piano lessons would interest you. Maybe you want to visit Hawaii. How about finishing the novel you started before the kids were born?

After I started taking some "me time," I found myself exercising and eating better, and as an extra perk I lost weight. I began to find the woman I had lost in the rubble of responsibilities. George I. Gurdjieff, a teacher and writer, tells us that, "In all ancient teaching the first demand at the beginning of the way to liberation was: Know thyself ..." I didn't know myself before my miscarriage. Even though sometimes I still wish our fourth child would've been born, I'm thankful to that little life for saving me from my backwards way of living.

We women tend to put aside the subtle, intimate nudgings of our inner self—sacrificing for others and in doing so giving up ourselves. The truth is, however, that by getting to know ourselves, we can be more to others. Your voice will take on a new softness. Your patience will not give out so fast. You will have more energy. Your family will be thankful for the new you. And you will fall in love with the new you. Jesus once said, "Love your neighbor as yourself," not love your neighbor more than yourself. Think about that for a while, what an interesting statement.

"Women are the cup from which everyone drinks; empowerment begins with loving and nurturing the self first—in order to quench the thirst of those who need us."

Marianne Goldweber

N = NESTING AND NUTRITION

NESTING

"At the heart of the cyclone tearing the sky ... is a place of central calm ..."

Edwin Markham

When my children were younger we used to go camping—the primitive way, using only a tent. It was a lot of work packing and unpacking everything, yet when the children were all asleep and I lay embraced in my husband's strong arms, everyone under the enclosure of the tiny tent, I came to the realization that everything I truly needed in life was right there. It is the most fulfilling feeling a mother can know. When I'm sitting engaged with my children in our nest on the couch I feel that fulfilling feeling all over again.

No matter how crazy the morning may become, when I sit down individually with each child a peace falls over each of us. It is a time of learning but also of that intimate closeness, usually only known when the child is younger. The television is off. The children know I will not be answering the phone unless it's an emergency. There is peace. Before modern conveniences and technology humankind had this unique closeness to one another. Can you imagine what it must have been like with only a coal oil lamp and a book to entertain the whole family?

Our morning school time routine usually runs like this: Children awaken at 8:00 A.M. They get dressed, make beds, feed animals, eat breakfast, brush their teeth, wash their face and begin working on assignments given the day before. By 9:00 everyone is deep into studies. I use this as a time to make phone calls, do laundry, straighten kitchen, etc. By 10:30 usually one child is finished with his or her school work. Most of the time it is my daughter, Kristin. She is much more willing and organized than my sons when it comes to school. At this time, I lay everything aside from my mind and concentrate only on Kristin and her lessons. If the boys have a problem and need my help, they must come to me, where I am sitting in a most comfortable position with Kristin. Our feet are propped up and we are surrounded by everything we will need for her lessons. I will stop only to answer or help one of the other children for a brief moment. The boys will have one-on-one time when their lessons are finished.

We usually begin by reading out of their chosen book for reading. This has been such a fun thing to do together. We have read aloud everything from *Mother Goose* to the *Iliad* and the *Odyssey*. Next we usually go over the child's journal. Correcting mistakes and talking about what they wrote. We then take each subject one at time, the child choosing what the order of the day will be.

After each child is finished with his lessons for the day, I give them a hug and tell them good work or good job. Or something like, "I thought your picture of the knight in shining armor was really cool." Allowing the child to walk away feeling like he did something right is very important for creating a happy nest and love of learning.

"Love begins at home and it is not how much we do … but how much love we put into that action."

Mother Teresa

NUTRITION

"A house is not a home unless it contains food and fire for the mind as well as the body."

Benjamin Franklin

Many mothers today are so picky about what goes into their children's heads, but not quite picky enough about what goes into their mouths. Did you know that Dr. David Katz, a graduate from Yale University and a nationally renowned authority on nutrition says, "More children are harmed by poor nutrition than tobacco, drugs and alcohol combined?" This is a totally new concept for me because when I was growing up if you didn't drink, smoke, or do drugs you were believed to be in great shape. How scary is this next fact? The Bogalusa Heart Study states that by the age of twelve, 70% of children have the beginning stages of hardening of the arteries. The sad story is most of us already know that our children are not getting the nutrition needed to become healthy adults.

But did you know that if your child has a tendency to misbehave, it could well be linked to poor nutrition? A long-term study from the University of Southern California found that children who were fed poorly were more likely to be irritable and pick fights than those who maintained a healthy diet. This tendency increased as the children grew older, many of them developing anti-social and aggressive behavior when not getting the proper nutrition. On October 14, 1997, an independent group called *Natural Ovens* came into the Central Alternative High School, in Appleton, Wisconsin, and began installing a healthy lunch program, by taking out all synthetic flavors, colors, and preservatives. The results were astounding. No longer were students misbehaving, being expelled, carrying weapons, or using drugs. They were studying and getting along with each other instead. Google "Miracle in Wisconsin," and see the results for yourself.

A few years back I decided that I was going to become more aware of what I was putting into my children's mouths, so I took some classes on nutrition. Up until that time I knew we weren't eating the best, but I had no idea how bad it really was. My first day of class the teacher talked about all the drinks that were a "no, no." I raised my hand and asked, "If you can't give them Kool-aid, pop, juice, or milk on a regular basis what *do* you give them to drink?" She looked at me, with her head cocked and eyes narrowed, like only a teacher can, and said in a stern voice, "Water." Water? I had never thought about giving my children water. (In my defense this was before consuming a bottle of water was a popular choice .) Julia Child claims that, "Water is the most neglected nutrient in your diet, but one of the most vital." Did you know there is much more calcium in a bunch of green leafy vegetables than in a carton of milk. **CAUTION: Be on guard at all times and read labels.** Many juice bottles mislead you into thinking you are buying a healthy drink, when it is really filled with sugar and colors. Did you know, too much juice, even if it is pure juice, can make a child feel too full to eat the proper protein and other nutrients needed for early childhood development, and can also spike blood sugar?

From that one class my *thirst* for knowledge of nutrition grew. I started changing things little by little around our kitchen, and the children begged me not to go to any more classes. They weren't happy that Captain Crunch had sailed away from our cabinets for good. Starting slowing is the key to getting healthy. You could begin by limiting your child's intake of soda pop, or red dye #40. It doesn't matter where you start. Just start. Maybe instead of buying that bag of chips or snacks you could buy a watermelon or a cantaloupe instead.

Mother Nature is always the best and most nutritious place to find our food. It has been that way since the beginning of time. Can you imagine what a woman from a third-world country would think about our grocery stores? Would she be impressed or appalled? Probably a little of both. She most likely wouldn't recognize most of the pre-packaged items as food, and in many cases neither does you're your body. But I have to admit, convenience is really great and it makes life a lot easier. Many times I have gone to the grocery store and spent over fifty dollars on fresh fruits and vegetables only to notice at the end of the week the only items we ate were the bananas. This is terrible, but so many of today's fruits and veggies don't taste as good as they did twenty years ago, making them a less desirable choice. The reason for this is because of modern farming methods and the fact that fruits and vegetables are now picked before they have a chance to fully ripen. If you can plant a garden with your children they will enjoy the home-grown taste of fresh fruits and vegetables and learn a little science the all-natural way, too.

Many parents today turn to synthetic vitamins thinking their children can get their nutrition from that source. If you are doing this you really may want to reconsider. Did you know that undigested vitamins have been known to clog septic systems? That's right, your hard earned money could literally be going— down the drain. Even worse than that, a study in the *Journal of the American Medical Association* found an increased death risk when selected synthetic vitamins were taken to improve overall health. This study shows synthetic vitamins should be avoided.

Don't lose hope if your children refuse to eat healthy. Modern technology has come up with some all natural ways to bridge the gap between what they need to eat and what they won't eat. The way my family connects the dots is suggested by Dr. William Sears, an American pediatrician, who has written over thirty books. It is a whole food product, called *Juice Plus*.

I was skeptical at first but after reading the eighteen published, peer-reviewed, research studies done around the world, in prestigious universities and medical hospitals, I was a little more than convinced it would give my family the missing nutrition needed in our diets. Some of the findings in these studies were: increased antioxidants, enhanced immunity, DNA protection, less stress on the body when exercising, lower homocysteine levels, and even better blood pressure. The list goes on.

But there was the cost to consider. How could I afford this for my whole family? I decided there were a few items we could cut out at the grocery store and put toward our *Juice Plus*. Then I realized my children could participate in a research study, called *CHS or Children's Health Study*, by doing this each child could receive FREE *Juice Plus* for three years. I am proud to say that I am now a backer of this wonderful program and would be honored to sponsor your children. If you would like more information on how your child can receive this product for FREE, go to the contact me page of my website (http://www.laurahuber.com) I would love to help your family get on the road to better health. If you just want to find out more on *Juice Plus* check my website, www.lhuberjuiceplus.com.

Here is a small, informative, and interesting list on some of the reasons to eat healthier:

APPLES—Good source of boron, increases mental alertness.

CRANBERRIES—Have strong antibiotic and antiviral properties.

ORANGES—Contain natural cancer inhibitors.

PEACHES—Aid in calcium absorption.

BEETS—Enhance liver and gallbladder function, and help build up blood.

BROCCOLI—Helps keep cholesterol levels in balance.

CARROTS—Boost the immune system.

SPINACH—Rich source of antioxidants.

TOMATOES—Protect you against sunburn.

The Rockefeller Institute of Medicine tells us, "If the doctors of today do not become the nutritionists of tomorrow, then the nutritionists of today will become the doctors of tomorrow." There are many, many other fascinating facts of what these and other fresh, raw fruits and vegetables can do for you, so don't monkey around with the health of your family. Go out and buy a bunch of bananas today.

"The doctor of the future will no longer treat the human frame with drugs, but rather will cure and prevent disease with nutrition."

Thomas Edison

O = OBSTACLES

"Life's ups and downs provide windows of opportunity to determine your values and goals. Think of using all obstacles as stepping stones to build the life you want."

Marsha Sinetar

Who among us has never faced an obstacle? Let him be the one to cast the first stone. Obstacles come in all shapes and sizes, at all different times of day or night. They are not choosey about whom they visit. Be you experienced or not it does not matter. Many times their visits come at the worst most possible moments. Why is that? Maybe we are on the wrong path. Maybe we need a wake-up call to change our course. Believe it or not—we are *not* helpless victims floating down the river of life getting swept up in a powerful current. Obstacles are just places that we must maneuver our canoe around.

Anyone who has ever been canoeing knows that you can make a canoe do pretty much whatever you want it to do if you have the knowledge of how to steer it. However, one must keep a vigilant eye on the river watching for obstacles at all times. Even if you think you know the river well, you will never step into the same river twice. It is always changing. And so is the current of life.

Just when you think you are sailing swiftly along an obstacle is thrown your way and you must change your course.

To the uninformed or untrained paddler a ride down the river can be very scary and even dangerous. Someone without knowledge may think that the white rushing water flowing swiftly looks like a fun place to steer the canoe to make it go faster, but the experienced person knows the water just looks that way because it is shallow and is flowing over rocks. The rocks could become a hidden obstacle to anyone deciding to steer the canoe into what appeared to be rushing water. Riding down the river could then become very bumpy. You may even have to get out and push your canoe off the rocks, thus overcoming an obstacle. However, the experienced paddler knows that still water runs deep and is an easier path to take. Daniel J. Boorstin, a social historian and educator, said, "The greatest obstacle to discovering the shape of the earth, the continents, and the oceans was not ignorance but the illusion of knowledge."

Before Columbus set sail, every educated man, woman, and child believed the earth was flat. Their *illusion* of knowledge kept them ignorant. Illusion of knowledge is probably what creates most of our obstacles, not ignorance. When one faces an obstacle it can be a terrifying time. Orison Swett Marden explained it best when he said, "Obstacles are like wild animals. They are cowards but they will bluff you if they can. If they see you are afraid of them, they are liable to spring upon you; but if you look them squarely in the eye, they will slink out of sight." If you are still and think deeply about what your next move should be, obstacles may disappear or at least seem a little easier to handle.

Many of the obstacles we face when homeschooling our children are nothing more than reasons to change our course or direction. One of my friends, who happens to be a retired teacher, now homeschools her children. I have learned so much from her about changing course when necessary. Once I watched her rip out the pages of a new spelling book because it just didn't fit into what she wanted for her children. It takes a brave woman to look the expensive spelling book in the eye and say, "Be gone with you." Sometimes we think, I'm on this course, it's paid for, and I must stick to it. It can be scary to change your thoughts or the direction of your path. Many more challenging obstacles can overcome you, like my illness and eventual miscarriage (in *ME TIME*). Take time to re-examine priorities. It may be time to change directions, or your way of doing things. Use obstacles as a springboard to get you on the right path.

Remember that God gave us the power to choose. A power greater than any other living being on earth possesses. Use your power of choice to overcome obstacles, thinking deeply about how to overcome them, don't limit yourself with old thoughts or habits. Stare down obstacles and do not be afraid to look them in the eye. They may decide to turn tail and run, or at least slink away slowly.

If there is an obstacle that you need to overcome think about the men and women who have made their marks on history. All of them overcame adversity in one way or another. Abraham Lincoln beat all the formally educated men in an election for the presidency, Thomas Edison failed not once, not twice—but 10,000 times when he was experimenting on the light bulb. George Washington Carver, a former slave, whose mother was traded without him, became one of the greatest scientists to ever live. How about all those pioneer women to give birth along the dirt path leading to the west? Now that is an obstacle! Rosa Parks, literally stared down her obstacle, paving the way to true freedom for her whole race. Helen Keller, blind, deaf, and mute after a childhood illness, overcame many obstacles. She tells us that, "The marvelous richness of human experience would lose something of rewarding joy if there were not limitations to overcome. The hilltop hour would not be half so wonderful if there were no dark valleys to traverse." What a brave woman—deep inside so are you. The next time an obstacle is thrown in your path, know it can be overcome with deep thought and courage. When you choose to homeschool, no matter how good you are, there are times when tears will be shed. Some days will seem very bleak and you'll wonder if you should enroll your children in school as soon as possible. The truth is, no matter what course you choose there will be some obstacles. Power through, by moving them out of the way or choosing to steer around them. Soon you too will become an experienced paddler on life's waters.

"The majority of men meet with failure because of their lack of persistence in creating new plans to take the place of those which fail."

Napoleon Hill

P = PRAY, PLAN, AND PRIORITIZE

"Many times the words of our prayer are in conflict with the real desires of our heart. We pray for one thing when really we want something else ..."

Charles L. Allen

Did you know that wishing and planning require the same amount of energy? Did you know that only three percent of the human race is truly successful? What about the other ninety-seven percent? Do you think they just wish their lives away? It is said that most people don't even know what they truly want out of life. Do you? Do you have a good plan to help you achieve whatever it is you may want?

Praying, planning, and prioritizing should be at the top of every woman's list of things to do. Sorry to say, it's not always on the top of mine. Life happens. We get busy and soon everything seems to be spiraling out of our control. Did you ever stop to think about the fact that plan is before pray in the dictionary? I know for myself if I don't plan to pray, it happens, but maybe not at the depth I would like it to. If we are pursuing happiness, we must purposefully plan our lives. There is an old saying that goes, "Failing to plan, is planning to fail." Ouch! This really hurts. It's fun getting up and just puttering around with nothing in particular in mind to do for the day. Although, the truth is, I do feel much better when I plan my days, weeks, and life. If I don't plan and prioritize, precious time slips secretly away, and I have no concept of what I've achieved. Surely I've achieved something I ask myself. I was busy all month. What did I do with all my time? Hmmmm? When I plan things I know exactly what I've done and what I've accomplished—not only because it's all written down, but I have the outcome of achievement to show for it. When you accomplish one thing you've planned, prayed, and prioritized for, it gives you energy and confidence to accomplish more. You become like the *Little Engine that Could,* saying, "I think I can, I think I can, I THINK I CAN." Then after you've accomplished something you can say, "I thought I could."

When we decide to homeschool our children it doesn't mean that you no longer have to cook and clean. Everything else still needs tending, so you better make a plan and prioritize how everything is to get done. Before you start, pray for God's guidance to surround you and help with all this decision making. Free downloadable pages of my day book, *The Life Planner–Discovering Yourself and Achieving Your Goals,* are available at my website to help you get started.

You could put it all on your newest electronic gadget, but magical things happen when you write down exactly what you want to accomplish. For some reason it seems to become more important. It's sort of like house cleaning your brain. Once you write something down it doesn't bother you quite as much— freeing you from that nagging voice in the back of your mind saying, "Don't forget about baseball practice. Did you throw Eli's uniform in the washer? What's for supper?" All of this can be written down and prioritized when you decide to plan and pray. In *The Life Planner* only five goals per day are written down. I have found that if I write down more than that, *(and we all have much more than five things to do each day)* I'm not as likely to accomplish everything on my list. If you can't accomplish everything you wrote down for Monday, when Tuesday morning rolls around it will seem like you're already behind. If you are able to cross off all five goals on Monday, you will have a sense of accomplishment, and Tuesday will seem like you are starting out on top of things. You will be pleasantly surprised by the progress you make. Note. I suggest crossing out items with a red sharpie marker after they have been accomplished. For some unknown reason it just feels good. :-)

"If you don't have a plan for yourself, you'll be part of someone else's."

An American Proverb

Q = QUALITY AND QUANTITY

"Greatness, generally speaking, is an unusual quantity of a usual quality grafted upon a common man."

William Allen White

We've all heard a lot about quality versus quantity. Some people believe spending a little "quality" time with your children is worth much more than spending a "quantity" of time with them without the quality. After much research on the subject of quality versus quantity one must come to the conclusion that both are vital to a child's development. If a mother spends a minimal amount of quality time each day with her child the child is left with an insatiable desire for more time with mom. Once I saw an interview with Katharine Hepburn. The woman doing the questioning was appalled at one of Ms. Hepburn's answers and asked her something like, "Are you saying that a woman must choose between a career and her children?" Katharine answered her in that superior, shaky, English voice we all know and love and said, "I'm saying, you bloody well better." This did not go over very well then and would not go over well now.

Many women today are torn between home and career. Some feel they would love to stay at home with their children but are not financially equipped to do so. If you have chosen to homeschool your children hopefully you are not working full time. You can do both, just make sure to do the things suggested in the chapters on: *Me Time, Plan-Pray-Prioritize,* and *Rhythm-Routine and Rituals.*

To homeschool you must spend a quantity of quality time with each child. Each parent must decide for themselves what is truly classified as quality and quantity, when it comes to the time they spend with their children. Remember when it comes to your children every day, every hour, every second is precious. Is there a mother who ever lived that said, "Gee, I really wished I didn't spend so much quality time with my children."? I seriously doubt it.

When my children were toddlers we were always together. Sometimes they would stay with a babysitter while my husband and I went out for the evening. Sometimes they would stay with our parents if we were going on a short mini vacation. As they grew older they would sometimes spend the night at a friend's. Most of the time we were together. Now, if I'm not sitting down homeschooling them or doing something planned I'm mainly in the background. Can that be considered quality time? I'm not sure. I do know that when I was a teenager the only thing I wanted each day when I got off the bus was my mom. Even though I was almost grown, it was a comforting feeling knowing she was there waiting for me if I needed her for anything. Now that my two older children have jobs I see them less and less. Quantity of time seems to be slipping ever so quietly through my hands. If I want to spend time with them I have to schedule it into their plans. Looking back over the years with my kids I would have to say that any time spent together is quality time, but balance is needed. Parents must separate themselves from their children occasionally. The following quote sums everything up.

"Rather, for all objects and experiences there is a quantity that has optimum value. Above that quantity, the variable becomes toxic. To fall below that value is to be deprived."

Gregory Bateson

R = RHYTHM-ROUTINE-RITUAL

"Children thrive on rhythm, routine, and ritual, and so do their mothers."
                                                    Sarah Ban Breathnach

As much as I am for the "free spirit" in all of us, when you decide to have children—especially if you homeschool them, your days need some sort of rhythm and routine. Take a good, hard look at how you spend your time. What's working? What's not working? Are there things you want to do but just can't seem to fit it all in a day's time? Figuring out how you want to spend your days could be one of the most important things you ever do in your life. In his book, *Think and Grow* Rich, Napoleon Hill tells us, "Resolve to throw off the influences of any unfortunate environment, and build your own life to order ..." Albert Einstein gives us his definition of insanity as "Doing the same thing over and over again and expecting different results." To get to the bottom of what is or isn't working; take a piece of lined notebook paper and fold it in half long-ways. Now title the two columns: Doesn't Work and Does Work. Next to what doesn't work—think of what might work and give that a try. You may have to re-evaluate from time to time to stay on top of things. For me, the seasons of life change just like the seasons of the year. Rhythm, Routine, and Rituals will keep everything in check.

If you want some different results, maybe it's time to look at how you spend your days. Rhythm is found everywhere in nature. Our days have a rhythm to them, too. **Rhythm is regularity**. Anyone who has ever been to the ocean knows the reassuring rhythm of its waves and gentle sounds rolling in and out on the shoreline. For some reason it gives a peaceful almost sedated feeling to sit on a beach and watch and listen. Regularity is comforting. It's a comforting feeling to know that the sun will rise and set at approximately the same time every day. Children want to know what is going to happen next. Sure everyone wants to be happily surprised once in a while but not on a regular basis. The Rhythm of your day should be for the most part—predictable.

Routine is nothing more than habits. Someone once said, "Bad habits are like a comfortable bed, easy to get into but hard to get out of." What are the habits that designate your day? Do you get up in the morning excited and ready, or do you sleep in and feel like you're running behind all day long? We are creatures of habit. That's why once you get into the habit of doing something it becomes automatic and easier. It was once believed that it took only twenty-one days to form a habit. Now science tells us that sixty-six days is more realistic. After twenty-one days we have confidence that we can do it, but it takes sixty-six days to make the habit stick. If you want to get into a good homeschooling routine be advised that after the first two months of routine and rhythm it gets much easier. After that everyone in the family knows what to do and how to do it. Having a routine will give your children a sense of security and trust. Not only does a routine aid in a child's development academically, emotionally and socially, but it will also keep his or her mind focused as well.

Rituals are customs and traditions. Customs and traditions are those fun things we do that change up the regular routine a bit. Rituals are in the rhythm and routine of our lives, but they are the unique deeds we do to make life special for our individual families.

It can be as ordinary as praying before every meal. It can be as different as bringing in a live tree for the family to decorate at Christmas. By creating some special rituals for your routine you will make some momentous memories for your children to remember and look back on with a sigh of nostalgia. In the chapter titled, *Fun Fridays*, I describe how everyone in our family looks forward to pizza night. Find some things you think your family would enjoy doing together and create some ritualistic customs. Fit them into the rhythm and routine of your daily life—you won't regret it. You can find more ideas and rituals to incorporate into your family life on my website and in my calendar book, *The Life Planner*.

"By incorporating routine, rhythm, and ritual into your daily life, many happy moments and memories will flower."

Sarah Ban Breathnach

S = STICK TOGETHER

"And if a house be divided against itself, that house cannot stand."
                                                    Abraham Lincoln

My husband and I don't always see things eye to eye. We have had many disagreements and arguments, mostly because I have what I like to call "Momma Bear Syndrome." Momma Bear Syndrome is an instinctive, unthinking act to defend the cubs at all costs. If Poppa Bear disciplines more harshly than Momma Bear deems appropriate the claws come out, and Momma Bear is on the attack. Watch Out! This can cause confusion and disruption in the den. Parents must quietly go behind doors if this happens and talk about what is wrong or right. Try to find middle ground. Sticking together is very important. Sometimes it's hard because men and women see things so differently. Once a decision is made, go out and talk to the kids together. If a punishment is needed now is the time to explain it to the child. Let them see you are now on the same page. You must stick together, or your children and the outside world will—*wear you down.*

Our decision to homeschool our children was not made overnight, nor was it blissfully blessed by both of us at first. The idea was first introduced to us when my husband met a colleague's son, named Josh. The boy seemed so bright and out-going, able to speak and talk to adults better than any other child my husband knew. Every day he would come home from work bragging about Josh and the fact that his mother homeschooled him. I was really intrigued, but in my own small thinking brain the thought that I could homeschool my children never occurred to me.

When it was time to sign our oldest child up for kindergarten I was having a very difficult time. He was still so little and young; I just couldn't imagine sending him off into a world that didn't include me or his family. I prayed and prayed about it without my husband knowing how I was feeling. The year I was supposed to sign Keith up for kindergarten happened to be 1999. On Tuesday, April 20, 1999, the unthinkable happened in a high school named Columbine. Two high school seniors went on a murderous rampage, killing thirteen students. It sickened every parent in America and frightened every student who heard of the horrific event. My heart had been telling me for quite some time I should homeschool Keith, but being inundated with the culture and society we live in I just didn't feel I was qualified. I felt that he needed to go to school. Even after the tragedy, I still thought it best that he attend school. After all, that's what everyone else was doing.

But my spirit would not let the issue rest. I lay in bed every night praying for an answer. Finally, I expressed my feelings to my husband, "You are always coming home and talking about how well rounded and what a great kid Josh is. I thought maybe I should homeschool Keith." His answer echoed my own feelings of self-doubt and he said, "But you're not a teacher. Josh's mom is a licensed teacher." Sad and dejected I decided to sign Keith up for kindergarten.

I made arrangements to talk to some kindergarten teachers and visit some classrooms. First I would be going to the public school, and then to the private Catholic school I had attended as a child. Since my nephew, Ethan, was in first grade and attended the public school I would be visiting, I decided it would be fun if I could take him to school that morning. We started off around eight. It was a beautiful day, the sun was shining brilliantly, and I couldn't help noticing he would really rather be playing outside. He took me in through the front doors of the school into what I perceived as total pandemonium. Having attended a Catholic school all my life, I had never witnessed children running from here to there in the hallways. I put it aside because Ethan was excited about me purchasing a mechanical pencil for him to use that day. After visiting with a kindergarten teacher, I was more confused than ever. I told her I had been considering homeschooling and asked her opinion, expecting her to convince me sending my children to school was the best thing for them. She answered me honestly saying, "If you can homeschool, your children will be better off. My sister homeschools her children. She offers them way more than any teacher could." This was a lot to consider.

Next it was off to my old alma mater. Here the children were treated totally the opposite of what I had witnessed at the public school. Discipline ruled as the kids walked out of church in quiet lines like little soldiers. Neither school was what I wanted for *my* children.

Perplexed and confused I went to a store before going home. As I was making my purchase the woman behind the counter asked me in a shocked voice, "Have you heard about the bomb threat at Brookville Elementary School?" All I could see was my precious, little blond headed, blue-eyed nephew whom I had just dropped off less than an hour ago. My heart aching and my stomach churning, I longed to go back into the school and pick him up and take him back to his safe home, but this was not in my authority. I had no right to do that. Only his parents could. I did, however, have a say about my own children.

That afternoon I called a neighbor who homeschools her children. She is not a licensed teacher and her children were learning just like everyone else's children. It could be done. I approached my husband that night about how I was feeling. The shootings. The threats of bombings. The pandemonium. The discipline. The words of the kindergarten teacher. He took a long deep breath and said he would think about it. We were both unsure, but we both agreed that no matter what we decided to do, we would stick together on our decision. Supporting each other through thick and thin.

Finally we both agreed that we would give homeschooling a try, at least through Keith's first year of kindergarten. After that, each year we would re-evaluate making sure we were doing the right thing. Back in 1999 if you were homeschooling your child many people questioned your motives and the well-being of the child. Some people were supportive, some were not. One thing is for sure, when you decide to homeschool your children, many people become experts in giving advice on raising them, even if their kids didn't turn out to be successful well-rounded adults, they now know what is best for yours. Even if a person doesn't have any kids, some still think they know what's best for yours.

That happened to me a lot back then. I took most of the flack because I am the children's primary care giver, and my husband is the bread winner. He always seemed to be at work or in another room when people questioned me. Sometimes I felt as if I had to defend my position like Grant defending the Union. But my husband, Bryon, always had my back, and if someone would sneak in from the left flank when my defenses were down—he was on guard and there to protect me. Once a close friend of Bryon's was questioning me about homeschooling after Bryon went out of the room. He was getting madder and madder at the fact that we weren't sending Keith to school; not now and not any time in the near future. Neither of us knew that Bryon could hear his every word. I was feeling overwhelmed and was really getting upset, when Bryon came in like the knight in shining armor he always is for me. He sat down banging his fist on the table and saying, in a rather commanding voice, "If anyone has anything to say about our decision to homeschool, they need to come to me and I will answer any questions they may have." No one questioned us much after that. Everyone knew we had made a decision and were sticking together and sticking to it. This meant more to me than words can say. It gave me confidence in myself, our decision, and our marriage.

Each of us is a different individual raised in different home environments with a variety of discipline techniques and belief systems. When you marry and have a family you must take the best from both sides and leave the rest rumbling behind, creating new values and new ideas. George Washington once said, "I have always considered marriage as the most interesting event of one's life, the foundation of happiness or misery." Keep a loving and respectful open mind toward your spouse's views and opinions. Encourage him to do the same for you and you're most likely to experience happiness and not misery. The country music song by Diamond Rio, *Meet in the Middle*, tells us how to stick together and avoid arguments. It goes like this, "I'd start walking your way, you'd start walking mine. We'd meet in the middle 'neath that old Georgia pine." Sometimes, it's not quite the middle where we have to meet. Sometimes one spouse has to walk a lot farther than the other. Once a decision is made, stand by your spouse. Be proud of each other. Your family will be much stronger and you'll create a home that no one can divide.

"Therefore shall a man leave his father and mother, and shall cleave unto his wife; and they shall be one flesh."

Genesis 2:24

T = TECHNOLOGY

"Technology … is a queer thing. It brings you great gifts with one hand and stabs you in the back with the other."

C.P. Snow

Doesn't the quote above sum everything up when it comes to technology today? A cell phone, a computer, a television are all great gifts to our modern world. Can you imagine how beneficial the cell phone would have been when Louis and Clark were exploring the north western part of the United States? "Mr. President. It's Meriwether. We've run into a problem. Is there any way you could send someone up to bring us more supplies?" How happy the gift of cell phone technology would have made a pilgrim bidding his family goodbye, before setting sail to the New World. Yes there would've still been heart wrenching tears, but they could have been comforted with, "I'll call you at the first site of land or whenever I get service." What about the solace a pioneer woman, living out west, would have felt if she could text her mother in Boston, "wht cn i do about deb's diaper rash? luv u:)"

Yes, modern technology offers us many gifts. Gifts we take for granted. But modern technology offers many vices as well. Television and the computer can be used as a learning tool for adults and children alike, but staying on your toes at all times is a must. You may be sitting down as a family enjoying a wonderful Hallmark movie, when a commercial will come on for some sordid sitcom making everyone in the family uncomfortable. I have found the best thing to do is either switch channels or put it on mute during commercials, because no one in my family wants to hear or see half of what is on the air. On the other hand we have enjoyed many shows together, and have learned a great deal watching educational programs. Nowadays you can pop in a DVD to learn about anything in or out of this world. The possibilities are endless.

Modern technology brought the once cumbersome computer into our homes. Suddenly the once seemingly rather large world became connected by the click of a mouse—and mouse took on a whole new meaning. But with this wonderful gift of connection, convenience, and education came many invasive and abrasive affairs. Children must be watched and chaperoned to make sure something that is not acceptable to your family's moral standard is not infiltrated by an unsuspecting child. Even vigilant adults can be tricked into viewing something they really don't want to see. Once my youngest son and I were looking up exotic animals of Australia. Imagine my surprise when a naked mermaid slowly appeared on the screen. That was the only time I have been thankful for "dial-up." It appeared slow enough for me to get off the site before his little eyes knew what was happening. The innocence of children must be protected. I have often thought about writing my congressman to suggest ways that viewers could tell whether or not they wanted to click on a website. Ending questionable sites with .xxx instead of .com would stop some of the guessing.

Sadly, when it comes to technology we have to take the good with the bad. But if you are alert technology can be a safe, fun, and successful way to educate your children. Most every curriculum offers the option of video streaming or DVDs to teach your children without much effort on your part. Some states even offer cyber schooling, a form of online schooling that may even be free. If you really don't want to teach algebra or calculus this can be an ideal way to ensure that your high school child will get the education and credits he needs for college. When children are young the free public television channels can teach them phonics, colors, numbers, good moral life lessons and more. Speaking of life lessons, *Feature Films for Families* offers a wide variety of good family oriented movies without a hint of unsuitable material. The possibilities for home education are unlimited.

The internet is filled with fun educational and engaging websites, many of which even have free downloadable worksheets, games and even tests. These sites can be of assistance when you are busy with other children or chores or if you just need something to fill a gap. Here are some free websites that may be of interest to you:

1. www.123teachme.com This website offers free Spanish lessons in a fun way.

2. www.starfall.com This website offers children an interactive way to learn phonics. I was impressed at the games and other education that was incorporated, like art, poetry, music, and even some Greek classics.

3. www.kidsknowit.com This website offers everything imaginable on education. The site is a little too busy for me but the content is great.

4. www.pbskids.com This site is mainly geared for preschool and kindergarten, but older children may learn something too.

5. www.free.ed.gov This site is very impressive. It's like having every encyclopedia in the world in your back pocket.

6. www.rhlschool.com This site offers free worksheets on many subjects, for grades 1-6.
7. www.teach-nology.com This is not a free site but it really has some great material for all ages.

Do a Google search and see what you come up with; I would love to hear from you. Post it on my website, www.laurahuber.com, to give us all some more ideas. As much as some of us may dig in our heels and say, "Whoa!" to the technological age we can't deny that it does have its gifts.

Never underestimate the power technology has over your life, and never underestimate your power over technology. My father taught me a vital lesson, when I was only a teenager, but I never forgot it. He said, "Be careful when you do something that is just a little below your moral standard, because the next time something a little *more* below your standard won't seem quite as bad as it did before you let your guard down. And before you know it this old world will get ahold of you." Technology can become a gradual addiction for anyone. Gradualism can kill people. Teenagers are getting hit by cars because they can't wait until they cross the street to read or respond to a text. Really? How important is it? Many children, who are left alone and unsupervised, surf the internet hour after hour while mom and dad are working. Many young mothers are spending less time with their newborns and young children because of addictions to technology and we have just scratched the surface. Use the gifts of technology, but adjust them to a healthy, moral, non-addictive amount. There is a delicate balance we must achieve in living in the world yet remaining apart from it. Protecting yourself and your family against immoral invasions, or nipping addictive behavior in the bud when it comes to technology, will create a lifestyle that nourishes you and your children, bringing joy to all members of your family.

"The greatest task before civilization at present is to make machines what they ought to be, the slaves, instead of the masters of men."

Havelock Ellis

U = UN-SCHOOLING YOURSELF

"To act without clear understanding, to form habits without investigation, to follow a path all one's life without knowing where it really leads—such is the behavior of the multitude ..."

Mencius

When I began homeschooling my children I knew only one way to teach. That was the way I had been taught. With a teacher and a chalkboard. I had wonderful visions of turning my dining room into a "classroom." I knew of no other way. I had, like so many others, been taught in that setting for most of my life. Children were to sit very still for the most part of the day, listening intently to what the teacher was trying to get into their overactive, little brains. If anyone has a question, "Let him raise his hand." If anyone knows the answer, "Let him raise his hand." If one is teaching more than three children at a time this may be the perfect course of action. But if a parent is teaching one on one, this is not the case. I had to "un-school" myself before I became a really good homeschool teacher. Albert Einstein reminds us, "Education is what remains after one has forgotten all he has been taught."

In order to give you a little extra nudge into un-schooling yourself, you may be interested to find out how our modern day education system got its start. Have you ever thought about how the most common way for educating our children now, began? Most of us just do as we are told, and do what everyone else is doing, not really thinking about why we are doing it. It is very important to ask the question, "Why?" often and in everything.

At the start of the twentieth century and the Industrial Revolution, compulsory schooling (enforced schooling) was taking root. For many children who labored in factories, under terrible conditions, to help support their families this was a welcomed blessing. They could now be children instead of slaves. But big business owners were not through with the children just yet. They needed disciplined workers for their factories who would listen to authority without thinking for themselves. These wealthy men knew that younger children possessed a need to please people of authority and our modern education system began. In 1835 a man named Andrew Ure wrote a book called, The Philosophy of Manufacturers: An Exposition of the Scientific, Moral, and Commercial Economy of the Factory System of Great Britian.   In this book he states, it is "nearly impossible to convert persons past the age of puberty, whether drawn from rural or handicraft occupations, into useful factory hands." Being the smart men that they were, big business owners found that if children could be trained in the industrial (factory) system it would reduce problems later on.   Sad, isn't it?   Our mass education system, put in place over a century ago, was not to bring out the very best in every individual child, but rather to make good factory workers.

By the late 1960's and early 1970's some people like John Holt, fifth grade school teacher and later founder of the modern day homeschool movement, realized the oppressive effects compulsory schooling was having on our children. His ten-year-old pupils were for the most part, scared and shy compared to the adventurous babies and toddlers he knew outside the classroom. He sums things up saying, "Education ... now seems to me perhaps the most authoritarian and dangerous of all social inventions of mankind. It is the deepest foundation of the modern slave state, in which most people feel themselves to be nothing but producers, consumers, spectators and 'fans,' driven more and more in all parts of their lives by greed, envy, and fear. My concern is not to improve education, but to do away with it, to end the ugly and antihuman business of people-shaping and allow people to shape themselves." Think about that quote for a while. Do you know anyone who is a productive producer, a consuming consumer, or a fanatical fan? It might be you. There is nothing wrong with these qualities as long as you love yourself and this is who you really are and want to be, however, if it is from counter-productive, indoctrinated teachings, you may want to think about who you *really* are and what you *really* want to be.

Today for many children compulsory schooling is still a blessing. Some would never be introduced to the subjects and people modern day education brings into their lives, not to mention meals that would have been missed at home. But for many children compulsory schooling is a curse, those whose minds are creative and active struggle daily with their duty of going to school. Sir Ken Robinson is to some extent our modern day John Holt. Sir Ken was a college professor at Warwick University, and was knighted in 2003 for his advances in art, creativity, and education. He tells us, "The fact is that given the challenges we face, education doesn't need to be reformed—it needs to be transformed. The key to this transformation is not standardized education, but to personalize it, to build achievement on discovering the individual talents of each child, to put students in an environment where they want to learn and where they can naturally discover their true passions." Do a *YouTube* search on Sir Ken Robinson, and watch his lectures; it really makes a parent stop and think about what we are teaching our children and why.

Sir Ken Robinson is one of the brave, non-conforming souls who declares that college does NOT begin in kindergarten. He even goes so far as to say, "Degrees aren't worth anything. Isn't that true? When I was a student if you had a degree, you had a job. If you didn't have a job it's because you didn't want one ..." Did you know that since 2001, according to the Bureau of Labor statistics, there are more unemployed college graduates than high-school drop outs? Back in the 1950's, 60's, and 70's only one in twenty people went to college. Now, one in three people go to college, flooding their places in the work force, after they graduate. These statistics are not meant to say that college has become unnecessary. This information has been given in order to rethink the way you think about educating your children. College does not begin in kindergarten. College does not even begin in high school. How many children at the age of fourteen truly know what they are destined to do in life? Some like my oldest son do, most like my other two children do not. By un-schooling yourself and honing in on those special gifts and talents of your children you will prepare them for a life they really want to live, not one that is dictated by society.

Many parents speak of college scholarships and degrees like the gold of Pizarro. Although these are both wonderful achievements, and deserve many accolades; there are other treasures in our children that demand just as much, if not more attention, than the accomplishments of sports and academics. It is a tough job trying to un-school yourself. The lessons taught us about getting an education are sewn into our very souls. We must take a step back from the teachings of our past and simply ask, "Why?" and "How important is it, really?" In doing this we can have an open mind to creatively educating our children, allowing them to grow into the adults they are meant to become.

"It is the mark of an educated mind to be able to entertain a thought without accepting it."

Aristotle

V = VIRTUES

"It has been my experience that folks who have no vices have very few virtues."
Abraham Lincoln

Although I cannot be as certain today, as I was as a child, that my mother coined the phrase, "patience is a virtue," I am thankful that she drummed into me what it takes to live a noble life. Today I wonder how many children are taught not only patience but the many virtues that make a truly honorable adult. The definition for virtue: a trait deemed morally excellent, thus valued. Personal virtues are one of the most cherished traits—especially when you're on the receiving end. Have you ever been pleasantly surprised at a random act of kindness from a stranger? If you have, that person showed a virtuous character.

Are you teaching your children the virtues in life? There are many different lists of virtues, going back centuries in time. The Greek philosophers Aristotle and Plato are given credit for writing about some of them. Later another list became popular, written by Aurelius Clemens Prudentius. If you do a search on the internet you will come up with many different lists all meaning or pertaining to about the same expression. With each virtue comes its antagonist. The Wikipedia describes the seven heavenly virtues and their vices as such:

Virtue and Vice

1. Virtue: Chastity—   Vice: Lust
   purity, knowledge, honesty, wisdom

2. Virtue: Temperance—   Vice: Gluttony
   self-control, justice, honor

3. Virtue: Charity—   Vice: Greed
   benevolence, generosity, sacrifice

4. Virtue: Diligence—   Vice: Sloth
   persistence, effort, ethics

5. Virtue: Patience—   Vice: Wrath
   peace, mercy, sufferance

6. Virtue: Kindness—   Vice: Envy
   satisfaction, loyalty, compassion, integrity

7. Virtue: Humility—   Vice: Pride
   bravery, modesty, reverence

If any of the above are missing from your child's curriculum, you may want to revise so as to include them.

A fun way to introduce the virtues to younger children is reading them fairy tales about brave men, women, and children who showed virtue by overcoming the many vices of the world, then have them act it out. Children love to be heroes. Acting out the virtuous life of another may not be as fun for older kids. They may feel awkward and foolish. Introducing them to some of the people in history who truly led noble lives is something that will astonish and encourage them into doing the same. It is the essence of the human spirit to live a virtuous life of purpose.

Keep in mind we can't be perfect all the time; with every virtue comes its opposite. Some people can get so caught up in what they are doing right that their virtues actually become a vice. A Greek proverb says, "The excess of virtue is a vice." A person can be so good at being humble that she denies herself her true gifts and talents. Or a person could dwell so much on doing right that they judge others who might not live up to their own virtuous way of thinking, and again make humility into their vice.

Striving to overcome the vices perfects our personalities. Gently reminding children on a daily basis what is morally acceptable and virtuous as my mother did, may aggravate them at times, but they will thank you for it later.

"Men acquire a particular quality by constantly acting in a particular way. You become just by performing just actions, temperate by performing temperate actions, brave by performing brave actions."

Aristotle

W = WE THE PEOPLE

"All of life is relationship."

Swami Rama

Sometimes when I tell people that I homeschool my children, then look into their face for a response, I can almost hear the music to the movie *Psyco* playing in their heads. First their faces get a horrified look, and then they ask the million dollar question, "What about socialization?"

What about socialization? From the beginning of time people have lived in groups and tribes, many clans staying in one living quarter with little or no privacy. Today's separation into groups, who are all the same age, has been unprecedented up until the modern education system was founded. Until that time, people lived and associated with others who were of all different ages. In families children are born one at a time not in litters. The older children naturally take on a more independent and teacher-like personality. The younger children learning from their older siblings, mimicking them, and doing things they may not have done without the incentive from the older more experienced kids.

Yes, they may learn some bad habits, but studies and research conclude children in mixed age groups tend to learn and evolve much better than those who are grouped according to age. Children who are grouped according to age tend to be more aggressive, depressed, and self-conscious, making learning and evolving into who they are truly meant to be a constant struggle. For this reason some schools are mimicking the system once found in one room school houses like the ones many of our parents and grandparents attended.

When my oldest son started playing pee-wee football, children were indexed into separate groups based on: age, height, weight, and years of experience to make it a competitive yet safer situation. This meant if the child was smaller he didn't naturally move up to the next level when he became a certain age. The practices were really fun to watch. It amazed me how much the younger kids looked up to and learned from the other older kids. Sadly to say, they have now done away with the indexing, changing the dynamics of the game.

Contrary to popular belief, good human socialization is not placing children of the same age group in a closed up classroom for most of the day. Children need to be able to run and play and associate with all ages from 0—120+. This way everyone learns and is entertained by one another. If you have a large family or are very involved in a church group it is still necessary to get children involved with others outside your normal social group. This will give them the social skills necessary to talk comfortably to all different kinds of people. Being able to speak with ease and comfort to anyone is an indispensable trait once you enter the work force, no matter if you're the owner of a business or an underpaid employee. Many times the way you can relate to employees and co-workers will determine how successful you become.

There are a couple of ways to make sure your child receives the desired social skills necessary for a happy childhood and wonderful life.

1. <u>Join a co-op</u>. A homeschool co-op is a group of people, usually in your neighborhood who get together on a regular basis. Every group is different. Our homeschool group consisted of at least eight families one year and only five another. Some families would drop out because their kids were graduating, some would join because their children were just starting school. Our homeschool co-op has dissipated now, but its lessons and friends still linger. It was a wonderful way for my children to meet people who were different from our normal social groups. My children started doing monthly oral reports in kindergarten. Starting a child out doing oral reports in kindergarten in front of a group of people who are of all ages really helps with public speaking (especially if you drill them the whole way to the co-op meeting).

We only met the last Friday of each month. Every year the mothers would get together in August, while the children played, to decide on a theme for the upcoming year. One year we chose geography. Every month families took turns making an authentic food, or giving a report about the designated country's religion, government, animals, etc. One year we chose the arts and put on a fabulous medieval play. The really great thing about this was how each mother was able use her particular gifts. Two of us wrote the play. Two made the costumes, and two made the props. All the children had such a wonderful time. We even taught them the Virginia reel, even though it wasn't a medieval dance; it was the best we could come up with. The fathers, grandparents, friends, and cousins were all invited to the performance. We ended the delightful evening with punch and cookies. It's amazing what you can do in one family's basement.

A homeschool co-op can open up a whole new world for you and your children. Talking with experienced homeschool mothers can be extremely encouraging during difficult times. You can guarantee that one mother in the group has dealt with the same struggles you are going through. If not, someone will know where you can get help. You may have to try more than one co-op before you end up with the one right for you. You may even need to start your own, but a homeschool co-op is an excellent social source for you and your children. Note: Mothers need a co-op as much as their children.

2. Enroll in an extra-curricular activity. See if your daughter might like ballet. Sign that young slugger up for baseball. If your child is musically inclined find an outlet for it. The possibilities are only limited by your imagination.

When you sign your kids up for extra-curricular activities, it opens their horizons even more, especially if it is something like county sports. Now your children are with many different kinds of people who have many different values and moral beliefs. As long as you and your children know what is right and wrong in your family circle this shouldn't be a problem, except in some extreme cases. Exposing children to different people outside your normal group is a good way for them to see why you and your family have rules and regulations. They will meet children who do not respect their parents or children who don't act with integrity. If they are like my children it will make them thankful for the wonderful example and home life that you are providing. Kahlil Gibran, a Lebanese American artist, author, and poet once said, "I have learned silence from the talkative, tolerance from the intolerant and kindness from the unkind. I should not be ungrateful to those teachers." I'm not suggesting that you drop your child at practice and leave, especially if he or she is young. It is best to stay close in the beginning, giving your child space enough to feel independent, yet know if there are any problems, mom or dad is just a few yards away.

Like anything else in life, homeschooling needs a good balance. Time spent at home should be more than time spent running children to and from activities. For our family we have found that if each child does more than two activities per year everyone gets overwhelmed. Remember kids need time that is not scheduled when they can use their imagination to develop their talents. Limiting kids to one or two activities per year will help everyone feel like a well-balanced family and still give your children the social skills they need.

"We the people" is the beginning of the Constitution of the United States of America. No one man or woman could have won the fight for independence by himself. It took people working together with a common goal. Each individual working hard for what he or she believed in, everyone contributing their own unique gifts for the common good of all. Homeschooling is no different. You can do a wonderful job teaching your child the foundations of education, but there is much more to life than book learning. Relationships are necessary to all human life. Children must be involved in some sort of socialization.

"We are all teachers; and what we teach is what we learn, and so we teach it over and over again until we learn ..."

A Course in Miracles

X = X it or not to X it?

"If you're not prepared to be wrong, you'll never come up with anything original."

Sir Ken Robinson

Did you know that a true artist can never make a "mistake"? A true artist can accidentally grab the wrong color, place it on the canvas, and create a thunderstorm instead of a beach scene. A true artist can see a mistake as an advantage and not a set-back. Picasso said, "All children are artists, the problem is to remain an artist as we grow up." Do you know of anyone who is not afraid of making a mistake? There are two different kinds of these people: One kind doesn't really care about his life. The other kind is very successful. My father once told me, "A scared man will never get rich." Meaning you must take the chance of making mistakes, and be able to rise above them when they happen.

Many children today are being indoctrinated with the idea that making a mistake is a dreadful deed. Believing it shows stupidity, carelessness, and negligence. Because of standardized testing and big red x's on homework papers kids believe that making a mistake is one of the worst things they can do. When in fact, making mistakes is the way we learn. Mistakes are the very basis of learning.

We all make mistakes. One of the many I've made was how I corrected my children's mistakes. I would get so frustrated at some of the mistakes they made when I first started homeschooling. Then I learned to lighten up and the funny thing is—they learned better and quicker. Instead of saying something like, "Are you kidding me? We went over that problem a hundred times yesterday, and you still got it wrong?" I now say things like, "Okay, let's see where you went wrong?" Then if it was a math problem we dissect it, "Oh, here it is, you added instead of subtracting." Trust me this method keeps many tears from mother and child at bay.

I still correct papers in red because I like to be able to see without searching the corrections that need to be addressed. Although it is necessary to show the child the mistakes he has made, it is more important to remember to praise him for all the things that were correct. A paper on, *Why I Like Summer,* may have a great number of grammatical errors but still be worthy of being published in a book of poetry. In the fourth chapter of Philippians, verse eight, St. Paul tells us, "… if there is any excellence, if there is anything worthy of praise, dwell on those things." Your words have incredible power. Be very careful how you use them. Give praise and help your children to learn from mistakes, so they can move to the next level.

Figuring out why the child made the mistake and addressing the cause will make it less likely to occur in the future. Children can become so frustrated with themselves; it is important for them to know that perseverance is the way to achieve good grades or anything else they may want to accomplish. Point out how Thomas Edison made thousands of mistakes, but because he didn't let them get him down he became one of the most important inventors of all time. Gary Marshall, actor, director, writer, and producer, who created shows like *Happy Days* and *Mork and Mindy,* tells us that, "It's always good to learn from your mistakes because then your mistakes seem worthwhile."

When it comes to learning from our mistakes, I like this quote by the famous, cowboy actor, John Wayne. I can almost hear his slow, deep voice saying, "Tomorrow is the most important thing in life. Comes into us at midnight very clean. It's perfect when it arrives and puts itself in our hands. It hopes we've learned something from yesterday." Showing your children how to use "true grit" to power through their mistakes, learning from them, and then moving on, will insure good work ethic as well as a brighter future for us all.

"The greatest mistake you can make in life is to be continually fearing you will make one."

Elbert Hubbard

Y = YOUR CHOICES

"If you limit your choices only to what seems possible or reasonable, you disconnect yourself from what you truly want, and all that is left is compromise..."

Robert Fritz

Many times we forget that in every single situation we actually have a choice. We choose how to respond to outside stimuli every second of the day. Can you wrap your mind around that thought? Every second of the day—in every single situation—we have a choice. A choice to feel and respond to anything that comes our way. The fact that you are reading this book is evidence that you are using or considering using a different choice than the majority of parents who have school age children.

When you choose homeschooling over the conventional ways of educating your children, your power of choice can really be challenged. Choosing doesn't stop with the decision to homeschool. It opens up many new choices and opportunities for you and your child. Now you must decide on the curriculum and content you want to use for your child's education. This can become an overwhelming and daunting task if you allow it. Everyone can tell you why their methods are better than everyone else's. There are thousands of different curriculums and ways for homeschooling your children. You could try looking over each one carefully, but the task would be colossus only confusing you more. Anyone who has ever been to a homeschool exhibition can tell you, "I'm so glad I went. I really learned a lot, but it was hard not to become overwhelmed by all the choices."

The best way to approach the question about what materials you'll be using is to think about what is most important to you and your children when it comes to learning. Do you need a structured plan, or would you like to structure your plan around your schedule and your child's needs? Is the appearance and layout of the material most important? Do you prefer a certain religious belief? Write down any details you deem necessary. Check it out, http://www.cathyduffyreviews.com this is a website that gives a summary on many different books by subject. It also offers free step by step online assistance during the curriculum choosing process. If you really don't have the time to sit down daily with your children, another choice you may consider is free online schooling. Surf the internet to see if your state offers this service.

When I first started homeschooling I felt that we needed to fully complete every page in each book or it would show failure on *my* part. But my ex-school teacher friend told me that the only reason they have all those math problems is to keep the class quiet and busy. She called it "seat work." I then started doing things a little differently. If my child knew all her multiplication tables it was time to move on to the next lesson. Most math books will repeat old lessons throughout the book anyway. I started assigning only certain problems, circling in blue ink the ones they were expected to do. Most of the time it was five problems from the newly learned lesson, and one each of the old lessons to make sure they were retaining everything.

I find lesson plans and unit studies confusing and time consuming. I have never spent the money on high priced all inclusive curriculums. I like to start the year evaluating each child and deciding on my own what would be the best for each individual student. Just because it says fifth grade on the cover, it doesn't take away your right to choose at what age your child could benefit the most from it, although it may upset your child to use a lower grade book, I've found that most history books and grammar books repeat everything year after year. The only difference being each year a little more information is added and a lot of pictures are taken away. To me this is discouraging because I'm all about beautiful pictures in every book. I believe they grab your attention and suck you in to find out more. One of my biggest mistakes in homeschooling was to get rid of the fourth, fifth and sixth grade Abeka history books. These would have made a great addition to our history classes in high school. Yes, the children have already read them, but how much information is retained? These books contain fun facts like how Florida got its name. (Because of all the flowers Columbus encountered upon his arrival.) Now their history books look more like encyclopedias. I can't help wondering if they would retain more information if I added some fun facts that they already learned over five years ago. I may have to try it this year and let you know how it works out.

As I said earlier I don't buy complete curriculums. I buy books based on these criteria:

1. How are lessons presented? Is it easy and quick to teach? Or does it go into too much detail?

2. Is the book attractive? Do workbooks look fun and interesting? Are the pictures in color?

3. Does it come with a test and quiz book? After the children got older, all I used for math practices was the quiz and test books. I found they really didn't need anything else and we were able to learn at least two lessons per day.

4. Does it fit into what I want to teach my child this year?

I've made my share of mistakes, and you'll probably make a wrong choice now and then, too. The important thing is to not get discouraged. It's okay. Ask yourself what would make this choice a better compliment to your child's learning style? You may just need to pass on a book or try to sell it at your next garage sale. Just remember you and your children are in control when it comes to homeschooling. Keep choosing. Keep improvising. If you're up to it, try using my eclectic style of teaching. It can really be fun. If you're scared you might not meet all the requirements; order a catalog from the company you're considering purchasing a full curriculum from. Before you spend all that money on materials you may never use look at your choices. Do you really need a teacher's book for history? Maybe you all you need is the teacher's book. Maybe you could get by with just the answer key for the tests and quizzes in this subject. Is it necessary to purchase all of those reading books suggested? Maybe you could go to the library and let your child choose what she wants to read. Just make sure you know that your power of choice is only limited by you.

"There are two primary choices in life; to accept conditions as they exist, or accept the responsibility for changing them."

Dennis Waitley

Z = ZIPPITY DO DA

"Memory is a child walking along a sea shore. You can never tell what small pebble it will pick up and store away."

Pierce Harris

When I was a child my mother was a very busy woman. She had four small children. We lived on a farm. My father had his own trucking company of which my mother was the sole bookkeeper and secretary, answering phones and making out invoices at all hours of the day and night. She did—and still does, wear all of these many hats with ease and grace. Amid all of her many duties Mom still found time to play with us.

One of my favorite childhood memories was walking out our long, dusty drive-way with my mom to mail all of the invoices she had made out the day before. It seems to me that back then the sun shone brightly almost every day and the sky seemed a little bluer than it does now. One time on one of these walks Mom taught me how to skip. Once on one of these walks she taught me the song, Zippity *Do Da.* I've never forgotten its happy lyrics. Whenever I think of that song, childhood memories come floating back to me like ripe dandelion seeds.

Another favorite memory was riding with Dad in one of the many different trucks he owned. My father was just as busy as Mom. He was running not only his trucking business, but also his farm. It was before seatbelts were mandatory, and I wonder how my sister and I didn't drive him crazy. Sometimes we would turn completely around and face the back truck window, seeing our reflections, and repeat no less than one thousand times, "The truck's goin' backwards. The truck's goin' backwards." He never got upset with us when we were with him. He always showed love and patience. Sometimes he would cleverly coax us into singing something different by teaching us a new song. (He still sings to us, and teaches his grandchildren cute little songs that he learned in school.)

Simple moments make lasting memories. Whether it was walking down the drive-way with Mom, riding with Dad, playing in the creek, mushroom hunting, bike riding, or learning to sing *Zippity Do Da*—these are the things that I remember of my childhood. Yes, I know how to read and write and I can add and subtract, but I can tell you very little about how I learned it. I couldn't tell you what the teachers did for me, but I could tell you how my mom taught me to write my name on our little chalkboard at the bottom of our bookcase, and how she and my father helped me cut out pictures that matched the letter of the day. I could tell you all about how both my mother and father would read to me every single night and the comfort it gave me. These are the memories of my childhood. What do you want your children to remember?

Making some wonderful, home spun, simple memories with your children is one of the best things you can do for their childhood. Don't get so caught up with education and duties that you forget to take some time for the things that really matter. Teaching your child to sing the lyrics to *Zippity Do Da* might be a memory to make today. Check out on YouTube, if you're not sure how it goes, and make it a — "my, oh my, what a wonderful day!" and a — my, oh my, what a wonderful childhood memory.

"It's surprising how much memory is built around things unnoticed at the time."

Barbara Kingsolver

CPSIA information can be obtained at www.ICGtesting.com
Printed in the USA
LVOW042003230512

283051LV00001B/3/P